Second Edition

Shopping for Shares

T0339278

Second Edition

Shopping for Shares

The Everyday Woman's Guide to Profiting from the Stock Market

Tracey Edwards

Wrightbooks

First published in 2006 by Wrightbooks
an imprint of John Wiley & Sons Australia, Ltd
42 McDougall St, Milton Qld 4064
Office also in Melbourne
Typeset in Bembo Regular 11.5/15.5

The moral rights of the author have been asserted
National Library of Australia Cataloguing-in-Publication data:

Author:	Edwards, Tracey.
Title:	Shopping for shares: the everyday woman's guide to profiting from the Australian stock market / Tracey Edwards.
Edition:	2nd ed.
ISBN:	9780730375043 (pbk.)
Notes:	Includes index.
Subjects:	Women--Australia--Finance, Personal.
	Stocks--Australia.
	Investments--Australia.
	Stock exchanges--Australia.
Dewey Number:	332.6322082

Cover design and images by saso content & design

10 9 8 7 6 5 4 3 2 1

Disclaimer

The material in this publication is of the nature of general comment only, and neither purports nor intends to be advice. Readers should not act on the basis of any matter in this publication without considering (and if appropriate, taking) professional advice with due regard to their own particular circumstances.

The author and publisher expressly disclaim all and any liability to any person, whether a purchaser of this publication or not, in respect of anything and of the consequences of anything done or omitted to be done by any such person in reliance, whether whole or partial, upon the whole or any part of the contents of this publication.

Contents

About the author

Tracey Edwards is your everyday Australian woman with a passion for the stock market. In just five years she went from having zero savings to having enough money to give up her boring 9-to-5 office job. She lives with her partner, Rodney, and two children in Sydney's northern suburbs in their second home.

Tracey created a set of 'investing rules' that proved extremely profitable and successful for her—easy, step-by-step rules for investing in both the long- and short-term markets that anyone can follow. A holder of an arts/journalism degree, Tracey has written articles for high-profile magazines such as *Bride to Be*, and many articles on finance and budgeting for couples. She has used her writing and investing skills to write two bestselling books and many articles to help teach other Australian women how to confidently invest in the stock market.

Why the stock market?

Chapter 1

When I first started thinking about changing my financial future for the better, the stock market wasn't the first thing I thought about—after all, I'd heard all the horror stories of people losing their entire life savings, and all that number crunching seemed a bit overwhelming. Even though I was pretty good at maths in high school, I remember very little of what I was taught then (has anyone ever needed to use an obtuse angle in their everyday lives since?). Anyway, wasn't it only rich old men with Porsches who invested in shares?

This was also about the time when numerous home-renovating shows started appearing on television, and it seemed that a bit of a paint job and a few strategically placed plants was making some people a lot of money. I seriously considered this as the money-making venture I wanted to pursue. In reality, though, I didn't have $50 to spend on a tin of paint, let alone a few thousand dollars (plus) for a deposit on a run-down shack that needed fixing up, so I abandoned my idea of becoming the home-reno queen and started looking around at other ideas. Saving and putting my money in term deposits and high-interest accounts sounded safe enough but — yawn — how boring does that sound! I was sure there had to be an easier way of investing for someone who didn't have a ton of money to start with.

I guess it was inevitable that I was eventually drawn to the excitement of buying and selling shares and I am so happy I did as it really suits my lifestyle. I don't spend hours a day stuck at a computer like I did when I was working fulltime. I probably spend an hour or so in the morning at about 10 am when the market opens (yes, I get to sleep in), and depending on how many stocks I've invested in and how active they are, another hour as the market closes at 4 pm. The rest of my day is filled with whatever I feel like doing: relaxing, pottering around the house and, of course, shopping. I enjoy buying and selling shares, I find it fun, so any research I do doesn't feel like 'work' — and I feel a sense of accomplishment as I'm doing this for me, not for some stuffy old boss who reaps all the rewards.

I wish I'd discovered investing when I was much younger; think of where I could be now if I'd started at 20 instead of 30!

So what's new in this updated edition?

It's now been five years since this book was first released and while my day isn't quite as laid back as it used to be (now, with two children, I rarely get to sleep in), I still can't ever see myself returning to a full-time job. As I say often: I make more money staying at home than I ever could working in a regular 9-to-5 office job.

The stock market still continues to be a good source of income for me, and over the years my strategies haven't changed all that much—although, if anything, I have far less time to invest in and research companies now. Today I adopt a much more relaxed approach to choosing companies and placing buy and sell orders—an approach I call the 'lazy girl's guide to investing'.

These days I realise that most of us—whether it's because we work, have a family or just lead hectic lives—don't have the luxury of spending hours trying to choose a great company, but still want to take control of our financial futures.

That's why I felt I needed to address a more relaxed approach to investing in this edition, one that helps you get through all the rough times that the investment market experiences (and, boy, we've just been through one of the roughest times in the market for a long while with the global financial crisis—GFC), but also one that reassures us that ups and downs are inevitable. More importantly, the approach will address what you should do when the ride gets bumpy.

I also wanted to answer some of the more common questions that I am asked about investing in the stock market—questions about investment strategies, companies and totally newbie steps to getting started if you have never invested before.

Hopefully you'll find that this new edition inspires you to make a better financial future for yourself by choosing the stock market as one of your roads to wealth.

Is it easy to start investing?

You know what I'm going to say—this *is* a book on the sharemarket after all. But honestly, I found learning about the sharemarket surprisingly less complicated than I thought it would be, and it doesn't take loads of money to start either. As you'll find out in the next chapter, I started with only $1000 and built up from there.

Once you strip away all the technical jargon, investing in the stock market really involves only three small steps:

$ choose

$ buy

$ sell.

It really doesn't have to be more complicated than that, and if anyone tries to tell you that you need to know about the current economic climate or understand the inner workings of the major world indices, then tell them to get a life. Because people know I invest in the market they often ask me what the current All Ords is doing. I have no idea what the All Ords is doing day to day unless I look at it. Since I don't own every stock in the All Ords I don't really care what it's doing most of the time. I only care what the handful of shares I own are doing. I choose (from research techniques I'll show you in this book), I buy (when I feel the time is right) and I sell (when I need to). When asked for a tip, I usually respond: 'Buy what's going up and sell what's going down', because it can be that simple, and that's all I do.

The gist of the jargon

All Ords: The All Ords (or the All Ordinaries index by its full name) is the Australian benchmark index that tracks how the sharemarket as a whole is doing (which is why it's the one shown on the news each night). It comprises about 500 of the largest companies listed on the ASX.

Another reason I like shares so much is that, unlike other types of investments, shares are relatively liquid. What this means is that generally it's possible to buy into a company one day and then sell it the next day (or even on the same day if you want). Try doing that with property!

It doesn't take a lot of time or effort to get in or out of a stock, and if you invest online like I do it's as quick as filling in a few details about what you want to buy and how much, and pressing a button. Or, if you prefer to use the telephone, you just ring up your broker and tell them what you want to buy or sell. The ease of buying and selling shares makes it less scary for me because I know that if I do make a mistake I can usually get out fairly quickly again by selling, hopefully without losing a lot of money.

All you need to start investing is an account with a broker (which is just like opening a bank account) and you're away. You're ready to start buying and selling into companies listed on the Australian Securities Exchange (or even overseas stock exchanges if you're that keen). It really is that simple, and *very* much like shopping, which is why I think investing in shares is perfect for all women. (I'll talk more about that in the next section.)

The gist of the jargon

ASX: The Australian Securities Exchange is the market through which all companies and many other investments such as commodities, futures and warrants are listed so that you can actively trade them.

Can anyone invest in the market?

The great thing about the sharemarket is that it doesn't discriminate. It doesn't matter if you're rich, have a business degree or pack groceries at Coles on the weekends. The market doesn't even know if you're male or female, short or tall, have brown or blue eyes. As long as you follow a few rules you too can become an investor.

I certainly didn't come from a privileged background or have any special skills. I actually grew up with very little money in a single-parent home. My mother once had to get food vouchers from the Salvation Army so she could feed us. Growing up in this environment made me want to live free of financial worry. At first I thought the way to do that was to get a good education, so I headed off to university and I studied hard, and afterwards managed to get a decent-paying full-time job.

After many years of working it seemed that I still wasn't able to get ahead. No matter what I did, I was still living pay cheque to pay cheque with meagre (if any) savings.

I fell into the common trap of believing that all I needed to do was get a good job and I'd be fine. But of course that couldn't be further from the truth. Living pay to pay is a dangerous way to live: anything can happen. To be free from this burden we need to get wealthy and have cash reserves or a nice little investment portfolio to fall back on.

So I started with only $1000 and eventually built up my portfolio enough so that in only a few short years I was able to leave my job and support myself with my investments. (There's more on how to get started in chapter 2.)

Yes, it's true that things were easy for me back then because I was investing during a great strong uptrend in the market that started around 2001 and continued past 2006 (it was all uphill for most shares). However, I also survived the recent fall in the market without much of a dent (I got out fast when I saw all my shares falling), and you can do the same if you know the signs.

Now I wish to share my success with my fellow women (and men, if they want to read about it as well). If I can do it, you can too! As an ordinary investor with no special training, I believe my strategies can be used by anyone, easily and successfully.

It's not as risky as you think

I'm not going to lie and tell you that investing in the stock market is perfectly safe and that there's no risk involved (if anything, the GFC has shown us that just isn't the case). On the other hand, shares don't have to be as risky as the scary news bulletins would sometimes have us believe. In fact, in the months leading up to the GFC there were many signs to indicate that stocks were overpriced and no longer good buys. I'll even show you how to spot some of those signs later in this book. And of course, people didn't lose money overnight. Most of the companies lost value over a number of months—plenty of time to jump ship and put your cash into safer options while you wait for good times again.

What is short selling?

Short selling is when you anticipate a decrease in the share price. You basically sell a stock even though you don't actually own it yet. You then close the short by buying it back at a later time. If the price is lower, you'll make a profit; if it's higher, you lose money.

Essentially it's the exact opposite of buying then selling. It's selling then buying!

Or, you could have sold short instead and ridden the wave down, as many astute investors did. Using short selling you actually sell a share before you even own it and then buy it later at a lower price, thus taking advantage of drops in the market.

Certainly shares are not as safe as a bank account but, despite the horror stories, the statistics are in your favour because you probably aren't going to lose all your money overnight either. Millions of people invest in the market every day and they seem to do okay most of the time. It's definitely possible to avoid disasters such as One. Tel and HIH and find true diamonds with only a bit of research. Did you know that both these companies had very high debt ratios and hardly any profitability? Even so, these companies didn't die overnight.

Stocks are rarely here one day, gone the next—they collapse over a period of weeks, sometimes even months. The savvy investor could have jumped ship long before such companies sank to their murky depths. Even stock market crashes recover eventually.

Over the long term (and I'm talking 10 years or so), shares make very good returns. In fact, the Australian All Ordinaries index has almost doubled over the past 10 years and, as you can see in figure 1.1, this takes into account both the good and the bad years.

Figure 1.1: over the past 10 years (even *with* the GFC) from February 2001 to February 2011 the All Ordinaries index has almost doubled in value.

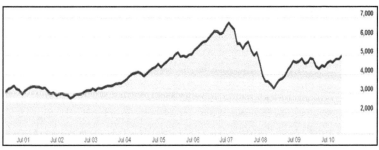

Source: <www.CommSec.com.au>

Living with market crashes

I just want to make a quick point here about market crashes in case some of you are still a bit nervous. It's true that there have been a number of devastating stock market crashes throughout history where the market has fallen extremely fast, taking many investors' money with it. The most recent crash—which as I write today (February 2011) is still in recovery—is the GFC. At the highest point in October 2007, the All Ords reached record highs at 6873 points. At the lowest point in February 2009 it was just 3255 (virtually half of what it was at the highest point).

You'll notice, of course, that this happened over a period of 14 months—not overnight. So, as I said earlier, with a bit of knowledge and a plan for what to do if your shares decrease in price you could have exited long before most of the damage was done.

Let's assume that you were completely unlucky and purchased your entire portfolio (including every stock in the All Ords) the day before the market started falling at roughly 6800 points. As I write today, the market is sitting at 4854—not quite back at 6800 yet, but certainly quite a bit higher than the low at 3255.

Now, historically the market usually recovers from a crash in about five years. The market recovered in only three years after the dotcom crash of 2000 (although some experts called this a 'bubble burst', not a 'crash'—whatever). The recovery after the October 1987 crash was particularly slow, but you still would have made all your money back by 1994 (seven years later).

While those seven years would have been worrying as you waited patiently for your portfolio to return to its previous levels, if you'd waited another few years until 1997 (which means you'd have held your shares a total of 10 years) you'd have made a decent profit, as the All Ords reached nearly three thousand points in 1997.

So, going by what history tells us, if you were unlucky enough to have bought all your shares in October 2007 before the GFC crash (and you didn't do anything to protect yourself by selling once they started falling), you'd only have had to wait five or so years — until approximately October 2012 — to get your money back. And if you have another look at the 10-year graph in figure 1.1, you'll see we're currently in a nice upward trend and very likely to reach that goal. So hang tight!

The gist of the jargon

Portfolio: The list of companies you own (whether you own one or 100 different shares)

Instead of looking at the glass as half empty, let's look at it a bit differently. Imagine that you decided to buy your shares *after* the shares had fallen — and you were incredibly lucky in that you managed to buy them at the lowest point (or when they were 'on sale', as I like to say). If you'd bought at 3255 points and sold today (just one year later) at 4854, you'd have a healthy 50 per cent return on your money! And goodness knows how much you're going to make in the future as the market rises again in recovery.

Now these two examples are kind of extreme (it's rare for anyone to buy at the absolute top of the market, or even at the bottom for that matter), but they show that this cyclical event is quite normal when it comes to share investing. However, if you'd had a plan, you could have got out relatively unscathed and even perhaps made some money during this turbulent time.

No-one knows when the market is going to crash or when it's going to rise to new highs, but my point is that, over time, even if you're unlucky enough to be involved in a market crash, if you're patient you will get your money back as long as you don't panic. That's the way it always has been and I see no reason why it shouldn't remain the same in the future.

Now for the good news

Even taking into account market crashes, the market historically makes about 10 per cent per annum. Did you know that even with a modest gain of 10 per cent per annum you'll be able to double your money in about seven years? That means if you start with $10 000 and you don't add any more money over the term, you could have nearly $20 000 in seven years, or almost $110 000 in 25 years, simply by keeping a lazy eye on your investments to make sure everything is running smoothly. That's definitely better than an ordinary bank account! You might even do better than 10 per cent with a little research and knowledge and, of course, a tiny bit of luck. As table 1.1 shows, all it takes is a bit of time, and if you let the interest do its work for you, you could have a very tidy sum after a few years.

Table 1.1: compound interest of 10 per cent per annum

Years	1	2	5	7	10	25
Amount						
$1 000	1 100	1 210	1 611	1 949	2 594	10 835
$2 000	2 200	2 420	3 221	3 897	5 187	21 669
$5 000	5 500	6 050	8 053	9 744	12 969	54 174
$7 000	7 700	8 470	11 274	13 641	18 156	75 843
$1 000	11 000	12 100	16 105	19 487	25 937	108 347
$25 000	27 500	30 250	40 263	48 718	64 844	270 868

While 25 years might seem a long time away, imagine if you put that money aside for your children when they were born; by the time they were ready to get married and buy a house you'd be able to give them a nice little deposit for their home, or if you don't have children it would make a nice little retirement bonus for you!

I bet you're starting to get a bit more excited now — and I haven't even mentioned dividends yet: the joy of receiving that nice, juicy cheque every six months simply by owning the shares. Yep, the company rewards you with cash for helping it grow. Nice!

Why is this book just for women?

When I was writing *Shopping for Shares*, I was often asked why it's specifically for women. Am I not essentially cutting out half my audience? Is the information in this book gender-specific? Am I some sort of hippie feminist man-hater? I hope not — to all those questions!

I think that anyone, whether male or female, can benefit from the information in this book and I'm sure (or I hope) that both sexes will be interested in it, but I specifically wrote this with women in mind because, when I started investing, I struggled to find a book with concepts written in a manner that I could easily understand, or that used examples I could relate to. The books I found were too general and skimmed over important topics that I wanted to know more about, or were complicated and took me too long to understand. A lot of the books I looked at — while they didn't come right out and say they were for men only — seemed very technical and written in a masculine style that I found a touch boring since I was more used to reading gossip and fashion magazines than finance books.

I know there are plenty of good beginner books on the sharemarket out there (I've even listed a few of my favourites in chapter 11), but essentially I wanted to write the guide that I'd love to have had when I was starting out: a guide written in the easy-to-follow, conversational style I was used to as a woman. I wanted a no-nonsense book that explained everything in detail, from how much money I needed to start with, to what to look for in a company, to—and women will relate to this—helping me through not only what to do but also how it *feels* when shares I buy go up or down. No book I had ever read explained to me how it would *feel* to put your money in the market. I hope I've created that guide for you, and that you'll be able to reap the rewards and knowledge much sooner than I was able to—and even beat me in the time it takes you to start making a profit.

Women make better investors than men!

Okay, so that's probably a bit of a generalised statement (and slightly biased on my part, with me being a girl and all), but the facts certainly seem to support it. Here are some references to back up my statement:

- In a British study of more than 100 000 portfolios, women clearly outperformed men, with the average woman's share portfolio growing by 17 per cent over one year, compared with the average man's share portfolio growing by just 11 per cent. ('Women invest better than men', *The Independent*, 16 June 2005).

- In a study covering the years 1991 to 1997, finance experts at the University of California found that women's portfolios gained 1.4 per cent more than men's portfolios and that not only do women outperform men in their portfolios, but they're also likely to lose much less during market falls because they're savvy enough to get out early. Furthermore, single women seemed to do 2.3 per cent better than the single men in the study. (Brad Barber and Terrance Odean, University of California, 1991–97).

$ Merrill Lynch agrees with this and has said, 'Women are far less likely than men to hold a losing investment too long or wait too long to sell a winning investment'. The same survey found that women are less likely to make the same mistake twice, allowing them to improve their returns over time as they learned what worked for them and what didn't. (2005 Merrill Lynch Investment Managers Survey: <www.ml.com/media/47547.pdf>).

$ In Australia, Professor John Price of the UNSW School of Mathematics also agrees that women are better than men at playing the stock market. He says the reason for this is that 'men's overconfidence [means] they tend to hold more risky portfolios than women. Women prefer to hold stock in larger, reliable companies they are familiar with'. (November 2000).

Pretty convincing statistics. The question should be, 'Why *not* the sharemarket?' Why not indeed!

Women are ready to invest

It's true. In the last few shareholder surveys the Australian Securities Exchange (ASX) has undertaken, it has found that direct share ownership among women has increased at a phenomenal rate. According to the ASX, the number of women investing in the stock market has doubled, and now women investors represent nearly half of all individual shareholders. How cool is that? Finally there's something in which we're (almost) equal to men.

If you check out any bookstore, the number of finance books written specifically for women is growing all the time, and even magazines such as *Money* acknowledge that half their readership is female (and even the editor is a woman!). There are magazines specifically targeted to women's finance issues, and even big-circulation women's magazines such as *New Woman* have sections and articles on money and finance these days.

Today's women earn more than they ever have and they're usually career focused. It makes sense that we want to take the next step and provide for ourselves and our families financially. It's so old fashioned to expect the guy to bring home the bacon while we stay home and watch daytime soaps, although if you want to do this it's entirely possible if you invest in shares (I manage to watch *Dr Phil* every day). It also makes a great career for those who work from home, whether you're a mother looking after the children, or you've simply decided to stay at home while your partner goes to work.

As women become increasingly financially savvy it makes sense that we want to learn more about what we can do to increase our knowledge of money and investing. The stock market is another notch we can add to our financial belt if we have the right knowledge. I believe all knowledge is important and the more we know, the more we can achieve. With financial security comes choice, and this is really what it's all about. We want the ability to save for a house or a holiday, maybe even create a small income while we pursue other interests. We want the freedom to be able to make decisions for our future and not have to worry about whether we have next month's rent or not.

$ $ $

It really is a wonderful time to get involved in the sharemarket. There's so much information at our fingertips and it makes sense that we want to be in control of our financial futures. This book is written for women who want to be more in control of their finances and have thought about investing in the market but are unsure where to start or what to buy. This is the book I would have liked to read when I was starting out, and hopefully it will help many women become financially successful.

There's no doubt that the information in this book can be used by both men and women. I use simple investment concepts that should work for most people, but I've specifically targeted women to show them that they can make a financial difference to their lives and don't need to rely on anyone else to do it. With financial knowledge comes the confidence and power to lead a happier and more fulfilled life and make better decisions about your future.

And of course, now that I've added lots of lazy-girl strategies for investing, things are going to get even easier! So let's get going, shall we?

How do I start?

Chapter 2

It's already clear that you're interested in the stock market; why would you be reading this book if you weren't? But maybe, like a lot of people, you still aren't sure whether it's right for you, whether you're even interested or what you need to do to get started.

Hopefully I can help out in this chapter. My friends often tell me that they would love to get involved in shares but have no idea where to begin. I don't blame them. When I was starting out I had no idea how much money I needed, or what was required to get up and running. I knew the basics, such as that I needed to have some money to invest with (yes, you can get away with having no money, but that's far too risky and complicated a strategy to begin with, so let's keep it simple), and I also knew that I needed an account with a broker, but how to go about setting one up was a bit of a mystery.

Fortunately, opening a broker account is really easy and not very different from opening a bank account (see 'Finding a broker' on p. 35). Other things you'll need are a computer and access to the internet if you want to trade online or, if you don't, just a phone will suffice (more on this in 'What equipment do I need?' later). But, of course, there's one main thing you need before you can even begin to think about investing. It's time to talk cash.

How much money do I need?

This is actually quite a complicated question because what most people are really asking is, 'What's the minimum amount I can spend to get the maximum profit from the market?' Boy—how long is a piece of string? It really depends on what you expect to get out of the market—the more you put in, the more you can get back.

You really don't need a lot of money to start buying shares. I started with only $1000 and built up from there. In fact, when buying your first parcel of shares you only need to buy a minimum of $500 to be a stock owner with voting rights and your chunk of the profits in the form of dividends. Sounds good, doesn't it? Well yes, in theory, although you do need a little bit more if you want to actually *make* some money in shares—otherwise your tiny amount will probably be whittled away by brokerage fees.

If we're going to be realistic, I'd say the absolute minimum you need is about three thousand dollars (preferably more if you have it lying around under your mattress). Here's why I recommend this amount: let's say you buy $1000 worth of shares and their value increases by 12 per cent in a year so you decide to take that profit and sell your shares. Let's also say that your brokerage costs are $30 per transaction (which is fairly standard for most brokers, although it's possible to find cheaper ones). Your profit for the year is $120 ($1000 × 12 per cent) less $60 brokerage ($30 to place the buy order, and another $30 to place the sell order). That leaves you with only $60 actual profit ($120 − $60 = $60) or just a measly 6 per cent increase (you could probably make close to that in many high-interest bank accounts nowadays with no risk). While it's still a profit, it's not really all that impressive.

Now let's say that you invested $3000 instead. Your brokerage will still only be $60 all up ($30 to buy and $30 to sell) because most brokers don't increase their brokerage fees unless you're placing orders of more than $10 000. We'll imagine that the value of your shares still increased by 12 per cent for the sake of comparison, and therefore you've now made a profit of $360 ($3000 × 12 per cent). Once we take out $60 in brokerage fees you're left with an actual profit of $300, or an increase of about 10 per cent from where you began. That's a lot better than the last example because the brokerage fees didn't consume all your profit; now you're actually making decent money!

Before you go off whining that you don't even have $3—let alone $3000—to invest, remember that I was in the same boat when I began. I had absolutely zero savings when I embarked on my sharemarket journey and I even owed money on my credit card and had to fix that first, so it's definitely doable no matter where you're starting from.

If you're starting with a healthier bank balance than I had then I congratulate you—you're already ahead of the game and you'll be able to get started a lot sooner than many others reading this book. You can probably skip the next section on budgeting to save up for the cash but, for the rest of you, this is where I'm going to help you save your first lot of share money. It's time to talk about budgeting.

Budgeting can be easy and pain-free

I know you're probably cringing right now and not looking forward to a lecture on how to budget and save but, trust me, I'm not going to make you write down every cent you spend in a little black journal or anything so I can then tell you where you need to cut back. Yawn ... how boring is that!

I don't want you to spend hours setting up a spreadsheet, although you might need a calculator. As you know, I like to keep things very simple, so all I recommend you do is divide your current income into three. Yep, that's it.

$ *One-third* is for all your bills and expenses.

$ *One-third* is your spending/play money to do whatever you like with.

$ *One-third* is for paying off your debts (if you have any) and saving for your first lot of shares once you've cleared all your debts.

While not everyone's expenses will fit neatly into this one-third method, it should give you a good guide on how to allocate your money evenly. This is the system I used when I was trying to pay off a credit-card debt and then saving up to buy shares. I think it's easy because you know exactly how much you have available to spend each week and exactly how much you have to save. Easy and pain free!

Let's have a quick look at a case study on Jennifer, who is interested in investing in the stock market but doesn't really have the money to start. She doesn't have any savings, although her weekly net income is fairly healthy, so she should be able to save up some money in no time.

Case study: Jennifer's mini-budget

Jennifer's income and outgoings

Weekly net income: $630

Credit card debt: $300

Car/personal loan: $Nil

Bank account: $20

Jennifer's easy divide-by-three budget

Bills and expenses (including rent): $250 (this is a bit more than one-third so we'll have to reduce the other two sections)

Spending money: $190

Paying off debt and saving: $190

Poor Jennifer has a sad-looking bank account (only $20—where did all her money go?), but the good news is that she doesn't owe much money on her credit card so she can pay that off in no time. She lives in a modern unit with her sister in a suburb of Sydney and shares all household expenses with her sister. Her share of the rent is $170 per week, and her share of the bills and food expenses totals $80 per week (not including her lunch money—that will have to come out of her personal spending/ play money; sorry Jennifer!).

As you can see, her weekly net income is $630, so by dividing this by three she should be spending roughly $210 on each of her three main areas: bills and expenses, spending and debt/saving. At present she spends a little more on expenses ($250—she does live in Sydney after all), so she'll need to reduce her spending and debt/saving amounts down to $190 each to even things up.

Yes, this leaves Jennifer with $190 a week for personal spending and, yes, I do think anyone should be able to do all their personal spending with only one-third of their income (or $190 in Jennifer's case). I think a trap most of us fall into is that we think we have more money to spend each week than we actually do. Once you know exactly how much you have to spend on whatever you like it's easier to budget. Jennifer could still buy a pair of shoes, some nice jewellery and a lush lipstick with that amount; granted it might not be designer quality, but I'm sure she'll get there in the future. After you start making money through your investing, you can always return to designer names if you want to.

With $190 going towards paying off her credit card first, Jennifer will be debt-free in only two weeks! Then she can start saving for her first parcel of shares. It will take Jennifer about four and a half months to save up $3000.

After that it will get easier and easier (she'll start receiving dividends and hopefully her shares will be increasing in value). In just one year she could hold nearly $10000 worth of shares! Nice start.

Jennifer's savings plan

Weekly saving amount: $190

Credit card debt: $300

Month 1: 4 × $190 = $760

Pay off $300 credit card—Balance $460

Month 2: 4 × $190 = $760—Balance $1220

Month 3: 4 × $190 = $760—Balance $1980

Month 4: 4 × $190 = $760—Balance $2740

Month 5: 4 × $190 = $760—Balance $3500

Month 6: 4 × $190 = $760—Balance $4260

Month 7: 4 × $190 = $760—Balance $5020

Month 8: 4 × $190 = $760—Balance $6540

Month 9: 4 × $190 = $760—Balance $7300

Month 10: 4 × $190 = $760—Balance $8060
Month 11: 4 × $190 = $760—Balance $8820
Month 12: 4 × $190 = $760—Balance $9580

Relationship budgeting

Often you'll be able to save up a lot more quickly if you're in a relationship than if you're single, because you'll have two incomes you can save from instead of one. However, not everyone's income is equal, so here's my advice for those in a relationship earning differing salaries.

First up, you should ditch the idea that splitting the bills equally is the best way to manage them. A lot of people simply think that couples should split the bills fifty-fifty without taking into account differences in salaries. Do you and your partner earn exactly the same amount of money? No? Then why are you splitting your bills this way? I believe both parties are equally important in a relationship—whether you earn a small or large amount—and thus both deserve an equal say in all things financial, no matter who brings home the bigger bacon. I recommend that partners should contribute the same *percentage* of their income to the joint budget.

This way even though the dollar amount is different, you're each contributing the same proportion of your income and neither party will feel ripped off. It's much easier if you open a joint account and each put your percentage of expenses in that to pay your bills from because then you don't have to grab a calculator every time the phone bill arrives.

Relationships are hard enough without bringing money issues into them. You need to do what works for you, but I think this method of splitting expenses is the fairest.

Case study: Linda and Marc

Let's look at another case study. This time it's Linda and Marc, who are married and have a small home in Brisbane.

They've decided that they'd like to get ahead financially and are curious to know what they could achieve in 10 years of saving and investing.

Linda's current weekly income: $750

Marc's current weekly income: $900

Combined credit card debt: $1290

Car/personal loan: $5000

Bank account: $3897

Weekly expenses

Home loan: $350

Food/bills: $250

Total expenses: $600

Linda and Marc have a little bit more debt than Jennifer (from our previous case study) had, but they also have more income, so hopefully they should be able to pay down the debt fairly quickly and start investing in shares in just a few months. Breaking up their expenses, personal spending and debt/saving roughly into thirds gives us the following:

	Linda	Marc	Total
Weekly incomes	$750	$900	$1650
Percentage to contribute	45%	55%	100%
Expenses	$270	$330	$600
Personal spending	$236	$289	$525
Debt/savings	$236	$289	$525

Linda and Marc need to pay their personal loan and credit card down before they can consider investing in shares. However, they've got a pretty good lump sum in their bank account already so it shouldn't take them very long. If they pay off their credit card and some of their loan with their bank savings they could knock their debt down to $2393, which would take only five weeks to pay off, based on their salaries.

At first they were a bit concerned about using their savings to pay off their credit card, but it's much easier to get ahead once you pay off your debts first. You're probably paying interest of about 16 per cent on your credit cards (and that's being generous—I've seen some with much higher interest rates!) and 8 per cent or 10 per cent on any personal or car loans. Even if you have your savings in a high-interest account earning you 5 per cent per annum, you're still losing about 5 per cent to 10 per cent per annum by holding on to these debts. It's far better to pay them off quickly and then start buying shares. I don't include home loans in the debt category because a home is an asset that appreciates in value and is not what I consider bad debt (such as credit cards and personal loans). You don't need to pay off a mortgage before you invest in shares (imagine how long that would take anyway!).

Once Linda and Marc have paid their debt off they could start saving for shares, and by the end of the year hold nearly $30000 worth of shares, which is a great position to be in after only 12 months. They could possibly own nearly $500000 within 10 years if they keep buying more shares with their savings and the value of their shares increases by a reasonable 10 per cent per year.

	Savings contribution	Total portfolio	10% increase for the year	End of the year
Year 1	$30000	$30000	$3000	$33000
Year 2	$30000	$63000	$6300	$69300

Year 3	$30000	$99300	$9930	$109230
Year 4	$30000	$139230	$13923	$153153
Year 5	$30000	$183153	$18315	$201468
Year 6	$30000	$231468	$23147	$254615
Year 7	$30000	$284615	$28462	$313077
Year 8	$30000	$343077	$34308	$377384
Year 9	$30000	$407384	$40738	$448123
Year 10	$30000	$478123	$47812	$525935

Don't you love compound interest! After 10 years, Linda and Marc will own more than half a million dollars' worth of shares, if all goes to plan. And that's after contributing only $300000 of their own money—the rest is the capital gain on their portfolio.

I understand that situations change: Linda and Marc might decide to start a family and have to live on one income, or both their incomes could increase over the years due to promotions or salary increases. But at least you have an example of what might be possible on even a modest increase of 10 per cent per annum if you both contribute to investing in your future.

Budget worksheet

Now it's your turn. You may need to make small adjustments, depending on your expenses, but that's really all there is to it.

Now you know exactly how much you have to allocate to bills and expenses; how much you need to save for shares or to pay off any debt; and, of course, how much you can spend.

What happens when your expenses are so much more than you can afford to spend or save? Not everyone's income is going to fit neatly into the one-third rule. But even if you only have $50 a week to spend or save you can still do it.

Your simple budget worksheet

_____'s budget

Current weekly net income: $_____

Credit card debt: $_____

Car/personal loan: $_____

Bank account: $_____

Now divide your main income by three:

Bills and expenses: $_____

Personal spending: $_____

Debts/savings: $_____

You may also consider either increasing your income or reducing your expenses. Is it possible to cut down on your expenses by reducing the number of phone calls you make or the number of takeaway meals you buy? Maybe it's even possible to get a part-time or weekend job to help even up the score a bit. If you still only have a small amount, don't be too concerned. Even $10 a week adds up eventually.

 The lazy girl's guide to budgeting

Now, while I know that my one-third budgeting plan is simple, over the years I've had people tell me that it won't work for them because their expenses just don't fit neatly into a one-third equation. In fact, living expenses have become so high today that it's quite unrealistic to expect that your income can be neatly divided into three, separate parts.

So I wanted to find a better budget—one that was more in tune with today's living expenses, but also super simple to follow. And, of course, it couldn't involve any complicated steps such as writing down everything you spend, earn and pay out (that's way too complicated for us lazy girls—or is that just me?).

I want you to take your net income and, before you do anything else with it, take out 10 per cent. So, if you bring home $1000 a week, take out $100. If you earn $750 a fortnight, take out $75.

If you take out your debt-reduction/savings money *before* you pay your bills or spend it, you'll find you won't miss it.

As soon as you take it out, you then need to either (a) pay off your debt/credit card *or*—if you are already debt-free (mortgages don't count)—(b) place it into a savings account.

Then the rest of your money goes to bills and expenses—and whatever is left over is yours to spend on whatever you like, without worrying about whether you should be saving it or not (because you've already taken out the amount you need).

Oh, and no more using your credit cards to rack up more debt during this time, okay?

There you have it! And you didn't even need to write anything down. Simple.

Saving for your first parcel of shares

Now that you've paid off any credit cards or personal loans, it's time to start your share-buying adventure. You need to save up your first $3000 to put into the market. Are you excited? Whether you have $50 or $300 to save a week, the real key here is *consistency*. It really doesn't matter how much you earn; what does make a difference is sticking to a plan. You can still do it on a lower income; it'll just take a bit longer. You know what happened with the tortoise and the hare: you might just beat the higher income girls to the finishing line after all. Remember that it's not what you earn but what you do with it that counts.

Even on $50 a week, you can still save for your first parcel of shares of $3000 in about a year. After five years you'll have a nice little portfolio happening. Won't that be better than where you were five years ago, or even where you are today?

So, how long will it take you to save your first $3000?
$3000 \div$ (your savings) $= (\times)$ weeks

Therefore, if your savings are equal to $300 a week, you'll have $3000 within 10 weeks, and more than $15 000 in about five different companies by the end of the year. That's a nice little portfolio. If, however, you only have $100 a week, you'll still have $3000 in about seven months' time to purchase your first parcel of shares ... and be well on your way to buying into your second company by the end of the year.

You can start with an amount less than $3000 if you wish, but remember that brokerage will erode any profits you make, so take that into consideration when deciding how much to start with. Maybe you'd prefer to buy using cost price averaging (a principle outlined later in this chapter) and build up your portfolio gradually that way.

It's going to take me too long to save up — I can't be bothered

I used to think like this. I'd work out how long it would take me to save up $2000 or $3000 on a small income and I'd feel overwhelmed. I didn't want to wait one or two years; I wanted to start *now*.

But it's amazing how quickly time passes and money grows, even if you're putting only a small amount away at a time. Even $5 or $10 a week adds up eventually, especially if you place your money in a high-interest account and don't touch it until you've reached your target.

Imagine someone on an extremely tight budget who only has $10 spare money to put away each week, and every financial year receives a tax refund of about $400, which they decide to add to their savings as well instead of spending it. Even on this tight budget, this person could save up $3000 and start buying shares after three years. Remember this: time is going to pass whether you invest your money or not. Which would you rather: a long time of doing nothing, or a long time of doing something?

Tips for earning extra income

Do you own a computer and have an internet connection? Cool—because I'm about to let you in on a few little secrets for earning income online, so you'll have more money for saving up.

Now I'm not going to promise to make you into a millionaire overnight, like those late-night infomercials do (oh, and please don't buy any of those as the only person who gets rich from them is the person selling the product).

I've been working (playing?) online now for quite a few years, and experimenting with different ways that you can earn money online. There are so many opportunities out there for anyone, even if you think you have absolutely no skill sets.

For example, there are some cool websites that enable you to offer to do something in exchange for money. One of my favourites right now is <www.fiverr.com>.

There are tonnes of people on there all offering to do crazy things for US$5. You could take a photo of yourself with a sign that has someone's website on it, write a 500-word article, read someone's fortune, predict the gender of someone's baby, or make a video of yourself.

If you check it out, you'll see the crazy things people will do for US$5. And I'm sure you could find something simple that you could do to earn yourself a quick US$5 as well. (Actually—technically—it's only US$4 since <www.fiverr.com> takes a US$1 fee for listing your gig there.)

Now, I know that $5 isn't a lot of money, but it's a start—and if you got five or six people a week paying you to do your thing, that's an extra $30 you could be adding to your savings goals.

Of course, if your skill set is more business orientated, there are places such as <www.elance.com>, <www.odesk.com> and <www.guru.com> where you can find jobs to do online (mainly writing articles, creating graphics or creating spreadsheets).

So, if you think you can write an article (the person listing the job will give you the topic and keywords to use in the article), the usual going rate is US$5 to US$50 per 500 words (depending on the quality of your work). I use these services a lot, and I often hire writers to produce articles for me for around US$10 to US$15 each.

If your work is good, you'll get repeat orders and you'll also be able to charge a higher price.

Generally, you could write two or three 500-word articles in an hour and you could make about US$30 an hour. Do one hour a day (writing three articles), five times a week and that's an extra US$150 a week in your pocket.

Think you could find some extra income to save now? Have a think about what you could do.

Benefits of buying shares over time — cost price averaging

There are benefits to buying a few shares at a time until you have the full amount you need. This is called *cost price averaging* or sometimes *dollar cost averaging*. It's basically buying shares at different times (when you have the money) and thus at different price points so that you buy your shares at an average price rather than worrying about whether you've paid too much or too little. It works like this.

Let's say you want to invest $5000 in a company but only have $1000 now, and it will take you two months to save up the next $1000, a further two months for the next $1000, and so on. Instead of waiting until you've saved up the whole amount of $5000, you decide to invest your $1000 now and every time you save up a further $1000 you'll add to your holding until you reach your goal of $5000. During the time that you buy into the company, the share price will no doubt be moving up and down so you'll be buying different amounts at different times — more shares when they're cheaper, fewer when they're more expensive. Have a look at table 2.1 to see what I mean.

Table 2.1: dollar cost averaging example

	Amount spent	Company price	No. of shares purchased
Month 1	$1000	$6.00	166
Month 3	$1000	$5.53	180
Month 5	$1000	$5.78	173
Month 7	$1000	$6.08	164
Month 9	$1000	$6.28	159
TOTAL	$5000	$5.93 (average)	842

Over the period of nine months, you bought into this company at various price points. When the share was at its most expensive at $6.28 you bought only 159 shares, compared with when it was at its cheapest at $5.53 and you purchased the most shares—180. Using dollar cost averaging, the average price you paid for this shareholding over the nine-month period has ended up being about $5.93 for a total of more than 800 shares.

Now, if you'd waited to save up the full $5000 to buy into this company, you'd have bought in month 9 at the final price of $6.28 and purchased only 796 shares ($5000 ÷ $6.28 = 796) since that was when you had the full amount saved. So, with dollar cost averaging, at the end of the nine months not only do you have 46 more shares, but also they cost you less on average to buy than if you'd waited until you had enough money.

'Ahh, Tracey!' I hear you say, 'You're forgetting about brokerage costs there. Won't they be much more and therefore the benefits of using this method be lost?' Well, yes, of course you'll be paying brokerage on five 'buy' transactions instead of one. But let's look at the shares again in 12 months' time, imagining that their price has increased by an average 12 per cent and you've decided to sell them.

We'll compare the two examples to see whether brokerage really makes a difference.

In both examples you'll see that the 12-month share price has increased to $7.03, which is the final price you bought at ($6.28) increased by 12 per cent. In example 1, you only have two brokerage fees (one for buying and one for selling), and in example 2 you have six brokerage fees (five buy and one sell).

Example 1: shares bought after saving the full $5000

Begin: 796 shares × $6.28 = $4998.88
One year later at 12 per cent increase: share price is now $7.03
End: 796 shares × $7.03 = $5595.88
Profit = $5595.88 – $4998.88 — $60 (brokerage × 2) = $537.00

Example 2: shares bought using dollar cost averaging

Begin: 842 shares × $5.93 = 4993.06
One year later at 12 per cent increase: share price is now $7.03
End: 842 shares × $7.03 = $5919.26
Profit = $5919.26 – $4993.06 – $180 (brokerage × 6) = $746.20

So there you go! Even when you take into account brokerage, buying a few shares at a time using dollar cost averaging will make you more money than if you wait to save up the full amount. In this example, that's even more than $200.

You're probably saying that it's all well and good when the share increases in price. But will dollar cost averaging work if the share decreases in price? Actually, there's just as much benefit if you buy a share that's decreasing in price.

Let's use the above examples again, but instead of the share price increasing by 12 per cent, we'll imagine that it decreased by 6 per cent instead. So this time the share price has dropped to $5.90, which is the last price you bought at, less 6 per cent ($6.28 – 6% = $5.90).

Example 1: shares bought after saving the full $5000

Begin: 796 shares × $6.28 = 4998.88
One year later at 6 per cent decrease: share price is now $5.90
End: 796 shares × $5.90 = $4696.40

Profit = \$4696.40 − \$4998.88 − \$60 (brokerage × 2) = −\$362.48 (loss)

Example 2: shares bought using dollar cost averaging

Begin: 842 shares × \$5.93 = 4993.06
One year later at 6 per cent decrease: share price is now \$5.90
End: 842 shares × \$5.90 = \$4967.80
Profit = \$4967.80 − \$4993.06 − \$180 (brokerage × 6) = −\$205.26 (loss)

Wow, even when you take into account brokerage, you've still lost about one hundred and fifty dollars less than if you'd waited and bought at the final price. You'll notice that the sell price is only a few cents off the average price you purchased at (another benefit of dollar cost averaging), so the majority of the loss here is simply brokerage. So there you have it: when you take into account both examples of when a share price increases or decreases, you're still better off with dollar cost averaging and buying your shares a few at a time. Your efforts to save up gradually don't seem so bad after all, do they?

Finding a broker

Before you can start buying and selling, you need to set up a brokerage account to transact through. As I've already mentioned, opening a brokerage account is not as hard as it seems. It's just like opening a bank account; you'll be asked to fill in a few forms, show some ID and then you're away. It doesn't cost you a cent to open an account, although some brokers like you to deposit some money into a special bank account (usually called a cash management account) for you to use to transact with. Often they'll even pay you interest on this money while it's sitting in the account waiting. Sometimes brokers also allow you to transact directly from your everyday savings account to make it even easier. I prefer transacting through my everyday bank account as I have easy access to the money whenever I need it and don't have to fill in any forms to withdraw it from a cash management account.

Types of broker

There are three main types of broker that you can trade through: full-service brokers, discount brokers and online brokers. Who you choose will depend on the level of service you require, such as access to research, help with devising a portfolio and ease of transacting. As you can guess, the costs of these services can vary dramatically, so it's important to work out what you will need. There's no use paying for a full-service broker if you use them only to place online orders.

Full-service brokers

As the name suggests, these stockbrokers are the ones who offer all the bells and whistles. They can offer advice and consult with you on which shares to buy. You can call and ask for any information that you like or ask their opinions on the companies you're interested in. Ultimately the decision to buy or sell is up to you, but for new investors it could be helpful to hear another person's opinion.

The main benefit of this type of broker is that they have access to data at their fingertips and they can often answer questions about a company or investment strategy quickly and easily, and guide you through your investment plan. Another benefit is that you'll probably get your own broker assigned to your portfolio, so you'll be dealing with the same person all the time who'll know your investment style and the level of risk you're happy with, and can therefore advise you on different strategies that might suit you. However, if you only have a small amount of money to invest with full-service brokers might not be interested in your business; they're used to dealing with people with thousands or even millions, so shop around if that's the case. You'll also need a full-service broker if you want to trade warrants or futures (see chapter 10) as it's unlikely that your discount or online broker will be able to place those orders for you. These brokers are usually the most expensive and can charge anywhere from $75 to $200 (or more) per transaction.

Discount brokers

Discount brokers are similar to full-service brokers except that they usually don't offer advice or help you with an investment plan. They are there simply to place your order for you. You'll still be able to do research and access information through them, but they won't guide you in the decision process. The main benefit of using these brokers is that they're much cheaper than the full-service brokers yet you can still get any information you want from them by giving them a call or checking out their website. There are many discount brokers who also operate as online brokers depending on how you place your orders (by phone or online), so this could be a deciding factor on who to choose. Expect to pay brokerage ranging from $50 to $100 (or more) per transaction.

Online brokers

Online brokers are the cheapest of them all. This is because you need to do most of the work yourself in terms of research to determine what to buy. While this may sound like a bit of a drag, I prefer these types of broker because I like to choose and make my own investment decisions. Besides, I can be a bit of a cheapskate sometimes and refuse to pay for things that I can do myself. I prefer to pay the cheaper costs of transacting online and do my own research. You can still get access to almost any research you want; however, you need to analyse the companies yourself to make sure they suit your requirements. Apart from the cost, the main benefit of online brokers is that sometimes you can place your orders straight into the Stock Exchange Automated Trading System (SEATS) without the need for an intermediary. These brokers generally offer the cheapest way to transact and you may only pay $15 to $50 in brokerage.

 The lazy girl's guide to finding a broker

Most banks these days have brokerage accounts linked to them where you can use your everyday savings account to trade from, making things much easier.

For example, if you're with the ANZ, you can apply to E*TRADE from the ANZ Investments & Advice tab by logging on to internet banking. If you're with the Commonwealth Bank you can register for CommSec right from the bank's homepage.

Of course, you don't have to choose the banks' preferred brokerage firms, and even if you're with another bank you can choose CommSec or E*TRADE (or any other broker you like the look of) if you want to.

Which broker is right for you?

Choosing a broker is personal and depends on how much money you have to spend and how much time you can devote to research. Obviously, the more time you can devote to making your own investment decisions the cheaper brokerage will be because you won't need anyone else to do the legwork for you (and that will save you heaps of money). You can also have more than one brokerage account. I know many people who have an account with a full-service broker for placing their complicated trading orders such as options and warrants, but do most of their everyday trading through their online brokers. Unless you already know who you'd like to transact through, I would recommend calling a few different types of broker and asking them to send you an information/application pack as it will be easier to choose one if you have all the information and costs laid out in front of you. The most important questions you'll need to ask are:

- ⚡ What level of service does each broker provide and what will you need? Will you be able to access share floats or IPOs (initial public offerings)?

- ⚡ What is the cost of transacting?

- ⚡ Is there a set price or will you be charged a percentage of your trade?

- ⚡ Are there different fees for different services?

- ⚡ What research will you have access to? Will you receive a regular newsletter about market movements?

- ⚡ What online tools are provided?

- ⚡ Are you able to set up watch lists or have access to live market data?

- ⚡ What charting tools are provided?

$ How do you place your order (by telephone or online)? Are there separate fees for this?

$ How long after opening an account with them can you begin trading?

$ Do you need to open a separate cash management account to trade through, or can you trade through your everyday bank account? If you do need a cash management account is there a minimum balance?

The gist of the jargon

SEATS: Stock Exchange Automated Trading System. Owned by the ASX, it enables users to enter their orders directly from their computer to the stock exchange's system for immediate transaction.

What equipment do I need?

You probably already have everything you need at your fingertips. I'm not going to suggest that you go out and purchase any special equipment, unless you want to. I'm also not going to tell you that you have to spend every waking hour glued to a computer screen, again unless you want to (and if you do may I suggest that there are more exciting things in life that you should try occasionally).

When I was starting out, I didn't think of myself as a professional investor. After all, I didn't have the latest trading or charting software, I worked from an old PC that had had its day and I hardly read the financial section of any paper (I much preferred the cartoons or the entertainment section). Everyone I read about who was involved in the stock market had computers that beeped at you at certain price points, and programs that devised complicated strategies and predictions as to which shares were likely to rise in price based on their beta or something … yawn, my eyes are starting to glaze over already.

The more I read, the more I didn't like what I was finding out. It seemed that these people were somewhat obsessed with the market, wanting to find the Holy Grail strategy that made them the best and richest investor in history. Some traders didn't even go on holidays because they didn't want to miss out on a few days or a few weeks of the market. How crazy is that. And try to get them to leave their computer screens between the hours of 10 am and 4 pm—nearly impossible. That was certainly not what I wanted!

While these investors probably have an edge over the average everyday investor like you or me, is making a few extra bucks worth sacrificing your life for? When I realised I was making decent profits using my simple methods, I thought: 'Why bother going to all that extra effort?' I'd much rather watch *Grey's Anatomy* than test multiple strategies for checking correlation levels any day. The old KISS (keep it simple, stupid) strategy was working for me and I still had loads of spare time, so why mess up that system?

I like to keep my investing equipment really simple. Here are the tools I use for investing, although it's certainly possible to get by on a lot less.

$ A computer and an internet account—so that you can research companies and place your buy or sell orders at the push of a button (if you plan to trade online).

$ A telephone—for calling your broker to place your orders, if you plan to trade this way. I personally don't use the telephone at all and prefer to place any buy or sell orders online, but others might like to speak to someone over the phone. Be warned, though: if you talk to a real person it's going to cost a lot more.

$ A mobile phone or email account—so that you can receive SMS alerts or emails when a company's shares reach certain price points. These days you can even trade directly from your phone if you have a smartphone like the iPhone. CommSec's iPhone app is one of the most popular in Australia right now.

$ Investment books—so that you can look up what a certain term means, or revise a strategy outlined by someone else. I like having my books handy in case I need to look something up quickly.

That's really all I use. I don't own expensive software or charting programs, but I certainly can see their usefulness. I don't own the latest computer, and up until about a month ago I was on dial-up for the internet. I'm now using broadband, which I absolutely love, but for reasons completely separate from investing. While everyone is different and investment styles vary, you certainly don't need to outlay a lot of money on equipment or software to start investing, especially when you're starting out, and anyone who tries to tell you differently is obviously earning a commission from the company selling the product. Try to use what you already have. If you look around at your resources you could find ways to invest right now without outlaying any money on extra equipment.

Do I have to be online to invest?

Of course not! People have been investing since the thirteenth century and I'm pretty sure there were no phones or web links back then. Early history has people meeting at a designated area to physically trade stocks person to person—the start of the stock exchange.

While the internet has been around for only 30 or 40 years, it started being used by the general public only in the past 15 years or so. Before that most investors primarily used the telephone for trading. A quick call to your stockbroker was the way most people used to trade (and many still do).

Nowadays we have the advantage of technology to make investing quick and simple. The stock exchange pits that I remember from the 1980s 'greed is good' movies are nearly all gone, with computer terminals taking over from person-to-person trading. I would have loved to see the frenetic pace of thousands of brokers and their assistants running around scribbling things on whiteboards and yelling company stock codes at the tops of their voices and, if I ever get back to New York, the NYSE (one of the few trading pits still operating today) is one of the first places I'd like to see.

Nowadays a computer's beeps and alerts are about as manic as it gets. Having an internet connection makes researching companies and placing orders so much easier. You can access new company information the minute it's released to the market, have emails sent to you if your shares hit certain price points, and buy and sell at the click of a mouse. However, an online account is not essential; a quick phone call to your broker will accomplish the same things, albeit only between the hours of 9 and 5. I can't imagine what a broker would say if you rang at 3 am asking whether Telstra was a good buy or not.

To start investing in the stock market you need only a few simple things:

$ *money for investing*—which you might already have, or be able to budget for

$ *a brokerage account*—which you can set up easily by filling in a few forms from your preferred broker

$ *access to the internet or a telephone*—so that you can start researching companies for buying and placing your orders.

Being successful in the market doesn't require large sums of money, a commerce degree or an expensive software program. If you have all of these already, great—you probably have an advantage—but there's definitely no reason why you can't start without them. No excuses—everybody has the ability to invest in the stock market if they want to. It doesn't discriminate based on financial status, race, sex or even intelligence (otherwise all your university lecturers would be rich and that's certainly not the case in my experience). As long as you follow a consistent plan and do your research you can easily become a stock market investor and be on your way to creating a better financial future for yourself.

Are you a long-term or short-term girl?

Chapter 3

Sometimes trying to figure out which method you're going to use for investing in the stock market can be overwhelming. Every book you read or seminar you attend claims to have the best and most profitable strategy that will work for everyone. I'd argue that if the strategy works for everyone and we all invest exactly the same way, who'll be making the money? Luckily there are many different investment strategies when it comes to the stock market; some are good and some are not. It's actually a good thing that there are so many different ways of investing because then you can choose the one that suits you best. I think the most successful strategy for you is one that you enjoy.

The first step in deciding how you're going to invest in the market is to determine whether you'd prefer to trade over a short term (holding the share for less than a year—sometimes for only a few days or weeks) or whether you'd rather have a long-term investing strategy (holding the share for many years, sometimes for even 10 or 20 years). I guess you could say that there are some shares you just 'date' for a while; whereas with others you're there until death do you part (or at least until a better company comes along).

When I started, I was strictly a long-term investor. I thought anyone who invested any other way was out of their mind and had to be losing money. Once I got off my high horse, I found that wasn't the case and there are many ways of making money in the market both long and short term. In fact, I used to do a combination of both long- and short-term investing depending on what the market was doing. When the market was extremely bullish, I used short-term strategies, watching trends and charting movements; but when the market slowed or turned bearish I returned to my original long-term investing plan and scanned the fundamentals, looking for great companies at great prices (don't panic, you'll learn how to do this later).

Nowadays, being time poor, I have reverted to more long-term investments simply because I don't have time to keep track of my investments or the markets. Also, I find watching the finance report on television completely boring. There are much better things to do with my time these days, such as reading a magazine, playing 'Angry Birds' and catching up on my Facebook gossip.

Often some of the most successful (and wisest) investors use a combination of fundamental analysis to choose which companies they like, and technical analysis to decide when to place buy and sell orders (see chapters 4 and 5 for descriptions of these concepts). Long- and short-term investing use different strategies to decide which shares to buy and sell and I'll give you my top tips for both methods in the following two chapters. But for now, it's time to decide whether you're suited to the buy and hold strategy, or would prefer to follow sharemarket trends.

The gist of the jargon

Bullish: When the market is trending up. Imagine a bull racing at a red cape: it pauses, waits and then runs straight at it again.

Bearish: When the market is trending down. Often moving much faster than when the market is bullish, it can sometimes drop quite quickly. Imagine a bear dropping off a cliff, plummeting down to the bottom of the ravine.

Finding your investment style

While short-term trading can be fun, it can be a wild ride and is definitely not for nervous Nellies. Likewise, some women will find long-term investing about as exciting as having to sit through *Star Wars* with their boyfriend ... again. It's important to decide up front which method you prefer because there's no use saying you're going to be a long-term player when you check the market every day and complain that your share's price went down 3 per cent on Tuesday. Likewise, you can't decide that you want to try short-term investing and then forget to look in for a few weeks—who knows what might have happened to your share's price during that time?

It pays to take a good look at what you expect to get out of the market and whether you believe long-term or short-term investing is better for you. There's no way I'm going to recommend you try short-term trading if you're convinced that the way to real wealth is investing over the long term. I don't want to try to prove that my beliefs are any better than yours, and it stands to reason that if you think like this then there's no way you'll be successful investing over a short term anyway—it becomes a self-fulfilling prophecy.

What I'm trying to say is that there is no right or wrong way to invest in the market. You need to find out what suits you best and what you actually like doing. While I personally enjoy short-term investing more than long-term investing because it's much faster paced and more fun (when you're making money, that is), I usually revert to long-term strategies overall. Perhaps that's why I was better at long-term investing previously and why I'm better at short-term investing now. Who knows? However, I still think it's important to diversify styles of investing as well as portfolios. And of course there's no reason why you can't do both at the same time.

You probably already have an inkling as to which would suit you best based on what you already believe or think you would enjoy more, but in the meantime take this fun mini-quiz to try to determine which investment style suits you.

Okay, so while this quiz is really just meant to be a bit of fun and not to be taken too seriously (I'm sure many long-term investors can still follow the latest fashion trends—Bonds tracksuit pants are still in, right?), it should give you an idea of what investment style you would feel more comfortable with. Do you like short-term investing or would a long-term investment plan suit you better? Which investment style suits you best?

Quiz: Are you a short-term or long-term investor?

1 How much time do you wish to devote to watching the market?

a) Every day—I love the thrill of watching my shares.

b) Once a week or so—I'm really busy but I can keep an eye on what's happening every so often.

c) Once a month or less—I've got better things to do than check in every day.

2 **Do you follow the latest trends or consider the classics a better investment?**

   a) Trends—I like to follow what's 'in' right now.

   b) Both—I'll check out the latest trends, but may invest in good basics.

   c) Classics—I like things to last me many years and still retain their value.

3 **How would you react if your share's price went down?**

   a) Panic—sell now!

   b) Be concerned—better keep a close eye on this one.

   c) Relaxed—the market is always moving up and down; I know I've got a good company.

4 **How would you react if your share's price went up?**

   a) Elated—sell now!

   b) Pleased—better keep a close eye on this one.

   c) Relaxed—the market is always moving up and down; I know I've got a good company.

5 **How would you react if your share's price didn't move after a few weeks?**

   a) Bored—sell now!

   b) Unconcerned—but better keep a close eye on this one.

   c) Relaxed—the market is always moving up and down; I know I've got a good company.

Answers

Mostly a's: You're a short-term trader at heart.

Mostly b's: Whatever takes your fancy, short or long.

Mostly c's: You'll probably suit the long-term investing method.

The main differences between long- and short-term investing

Have you worked out what you think you'll enjoy more yet? I suppose you want a bit more detail about each style before you make your final decision. The obvious difference is the length of time you hold your shares, but there are other differences when choosing stocks using the two investment methods.

Long-term investment style

$ *Research—only once or twice a year.* Most of your homework and research is done up-front either once or twice a year, according to how often a company posts its financial information. This information is easy to find as every company listed on the stock exchange is required to publish its financial information for everyone to access. It can be accessed online at the company's website, on the ASX website or directly from your broker. If you don't have internet access, you can call your broker or call the company direct and ask for their current annual report. The research required to choose your companies can take a few good hours, if not more. However, you can save time by investing in *Top Stocks* by Martin Roth. This book is published each year, and lists about one hundred companies on which the research has already been done for you. I find this book such a time saver and totally worth the money as the only companies listed in the book already fit many of the criteria I already use for choosing my own companies for long-term investing, such as low debt and high return on equity.

$ *Choosing your companies—fundamental analysis.* From this research you usually pick a handful of stocks that you would be interested in buying. Fundamental analysis looks at things such as the company's profitability, earnings stability and past history (more on fundamental analysis in chapter 4). Once you have the list of shares you're interested in buying you can just sit back and wait for them to hit a price that you're happy to buy them at or, if they're already there, buy them now. For long-term investing, I don't recommend simply buying stocks at whatever price they happen to be offered for at the time (this is different from short-term investing where the buy price is unimportant). Some companies that look great on paper are overpriced and you'll need to wait until they fall a bit before you purchase them. I use a set formula to determine the price to buy shares at, which I outline in chapter 4.

$ *Dividend.* The other main benefit of long-term investing is those lovely dividend cheques. Most companies will send their shareholders a small cheque every six months as their share of the company's profits. With short-term investing you can often miss out on these cheques unless you hold the stock at the right time. It's also possible to invest simply for the dividend cheques you receive every six months if you choose companies with a high dividend yield (think of it as interest paid to your account).

 Lazy girl's guide to long-term investing

If you want to spend the least amount of time looking at the stock market as possible while still making smart investment decisions, long-term investing is for you.

Short-term investment style

$ *Research — ongoing.* Less time is devoted up-front to choosing shares, but more time is spent watching them closely week by week. To work out which shares to buy, you can keep an eye on general market movements by watching the news and reading the financial section of the newspaper (this can be a bit boring so it's okay to just quickly scan this section). I usually look at which sectors are outperforming the others and from that I choose the best shares in that sector. Sectors (or indices) are simply the way the ASX breaks down the companies into categories. Companies can be sorted into categories depending on their size, such as the top 100 shares (S&P/ASX 100), or sorted according to what they do, such as energy stocks or industrials. Often they're broken down even further, such as S&P/ASX 100 Energy, which represents the energy stocks listed in the top 100 shares.

$ *Choosing your shares — charting or technical analysis.* After your research has narrowed down your selection of shares based on sector analysis or looking at the financial section of the newspaper for trends, looking at each company's chart is often the next step to take when choosing shares for short-term investing. Technical analysis, or 'looking at charts', is a good way of analysing shares for short-term investing. At a glance you can usually tell in which direction the share price is heading and its overall behaviour. A chart can give you lots of information on the share, such as its average volume (how much people are buying and selling), the way the share price moves (up, down or sideways) and the patterns particular to that company (the company's share price might have a habit of rising for three days and falling on the fourth day, for example). I've included some examples of charts in chapter 5.

$ *Volatility.* The main benefit of short-term over long-term investing is that the share price can often move quickly, which means you could make a decent profit in a short period of time; however, the reverse is also true, and your share might decrease in price just as quickly. With good money-management techniques, although you won't be able to avoid a share decreasing in price, you can avoid losing large amounts of your capital by cutting your losses early. This is the most important strategy when investing over the short term: cutting your losses early and letting your profits ride. I'll explain this concept more fully in chapter 5.

 Lazy girl's guide to short-term investing

Who says you can't trade short term and still be lazy? You know I've got some great strategies for lazy girls and short-term trading coming up, don't you? You'd better believe it!

Long-term versus short-term investing

Table 3.1 (overleaf) gives you a quick comparison of the two investment styles.

Which method will make more money?

Ahh, now we enter the biggest debate that has raged since the stock market started! Will you make more money investing over the long term, or the short term? I'm sure you've all heard the urban myths of the investors who double their money in only a few days with short-term trading (or the ones that go belly up overnight using the same methods), and the old white lie that if you invest in only blue-chip stocks on a long-term basis you'll be guaranteed to make your fortune. Umm ... isn't Telstra considered a blue-chip company? I think the only investor who made money there was the government (oops ... probably shouldn't have said that).

While you can definitely make money faster with short-term trading, there are some inherent problems.

Table 3.1: long-term versus short-term investing

Long-term investing	Short-term investing
Dividend cheques arrive twice per year for most companies.	You often miss out on dividends because you don't hold the share long enough.
You don't really care about small up and down movements as long as the general trend is up.	Share prices tend to jump around a lot, which you use to your advantage.
Long-term investing is a *waiting* game. You choose your stocks and wait for them to increase in price over a number of years.	Short-term investing is a *numbers* game. Not every stock you choose is going to be a winner so you cut your bad stocks loose quickly and ride the wave of the good ones.
You need to look at the company fundamentals before deciding on a good stock to purchase.	You don't need to know anything about the stock except whether it's currently going up or down.
It's more stable over the long term, and many would say much safer.	You try to take advantage of small movements in the stock to gain quick profits—more risk with more reward (if things go in your favour).
Once you do your research up-front you can sit back and relax without having to worry too much about your shares (you only need to check them about twice a year).	You'll need to keep a close eye on what the market is doing so you can react to upturns and downturns quickly.

The first is the capital gains tax concession that only holders of shares for one year or longer are entitled to. You're also likely to miss out on dividends (and the tax benefits of dividends). And then there's the cost of your brokerage — if you only trade twice a month that still adds up to $720 per year just on transaction fees! But with long-term investing you might be showing a loss on your portfolio before you show any profit. Are you the type of person who's able to ride that out without freaking out?

Knowing that your shares have decreased in price can be scary and it can be easy to forget that long-term investing has produced favourable positive results. Are you able to wait until the share price turns around again without acting impulsively? A lot of people can't use long-term investing successfully because they bail out at the first downturn in the market. They might think they're long-term players but are acting more like short-term traders, following the trends. Advocates for both sides usually have cute little sayings to back up their point of view. Short-term devotees might argue that 'the trend is your friend' and that's where the real money lies, whereas long-term players counter with 'it's time in, not timing, that counts'. So who is right?

The truth is that, with a good plan in place, either method can make you money if you're consistent. But, like everything in life, what works for one person isn't going to work for another, so you need to find a fit with your preferred style and one that you enjoy using. If you enjoy the method you use then you have a greater chance of being a success than if you don't. Just because Jimmy down the road recommends buying undervalued stocks and selling them six months later because that's what he did to make a few thousand doesn't mean it will work for you, so try on a few styles for size and see which one fits best.

Think of it as trying on that sexy little denim mini. It might look gorgeous on one person, but hideous on the next. You know what you look good in, so it should be a snap finding out which style you'd like to use in the market.

$ $ $

Deciding which of the two main styles of investing is right for you is usually a matter of choosing which one you feel most comfortable with and how much time you want to spend tracking your investments. Neither style is going to make you a millionaire if you don't enjoy the process. Once you decide which style you want to use (or maybe, like me, you'd like to try both methods), the following two chapters will show you my tips on choosing companies to invest in based on the method you've chosen.

Investing for the long term

Chapter 4

Have you thought about what you'll be doing five years from now? How about 10 years from now? Will you be married, living somewhere else, have children or be retired? Will you still be in the same career or even the same job? (Unless you love your job, I hope you'll have at least been promoted within those five years!)

Five years is roughly how long it took me to go from having no savings, working a dull, 9-to-5 job and owning nothing of any value, to being able to feel a sense of control over my financial future—and the sharemarket helped me do that. I can honestly say that I'm in a much better position now than I ever believed I could be five years ago. Bring on the next five years, I say—who knows where I'll be then!

Actually, as it's been five years since I first wrote this book, I can happily say that I'm still doing pretty well. Sure, my shares got quite a knock during the global meltdown but, fortunately—because I got out fairly early with many of them—I wasn't hurt too badly (you can learn more about how to do this, too, in chapter 8).

However, we're over that bumpy three-year ride and things are turning around again. And the *next* five years should be pretty interesting (and profitable) for long-term investors, so what are you waiting for?

Investing in the stock market over the long term has shown an average return of 10 to 12 per cent per annum. Even if you take into account those years when shares have crashed, historically the market still offers consistent returns for long-term investing. If you're careful and choose shares wisely, you too can profit like so many others have.

Invest like the best

Imagine you had a spare $105 000 floating around. For most of us, that would be a dream to start with, but then imagine that you were able to turn that into a $20 billion-plus fortune. Sounds impossible? Actually it's not; one of the world's best investors was able to accomplish this just by investing wisely in stocks. The investor's name: Warren Buffett.

He's an American investor—not Australian—but that doesn't mean we can't use his style to help us make gains in the market. When it comes to investing long term, there's no doubt that we can learn from the master. All he did was invest in reliable, big companies such as Coca-Cola, Disney and McDonald's. He ignored all the Wall Street hype; in fact, he said he didn't even care what the Dow Jones was doing day by day, just what his shares were. (You may find me saying exactly the same thing about the All Ordinaries index.)

His premise is simple: find a great company and never pay too much for it. In other words, find what every woman loves—a bargain!

Of all the investment strategies I've read about and tried, Warren Buffett's strategies are the ones I've based most of my 'rules' on.

This method of investment in the stock market is for those women who like nice, stable companies with no surprises. You marry these safe stocks rather than date them. These shares are your long-term best friend, ones that you don't need to keep an eye on to make sure they're behaving. As long as their financials remain great, you should be prepared to hold on to these for as long as it takes, in sickness and in health.

Time for some fundamental analysis

Stock winners don't just fall into your lap; you need to do a bit of homework beforehand so that you can narrow down your selections to find the perfect company (or 10) that suits your needs. But once you find the winners, they should continue to pay dividends and increase in value for as long as you hold them.

But how do you find them to start with? It's time to learn a little fundamental analysis. But don't worry — it's not nearly as complicated as your accountant will make out. Besides, it has the word 'fun' in it, so how bad can it be?

Fundamental analysis is basically looking at companies' financials (their balance sheets, and their profit and loss statements) to determine which of them are healthy and robust and which are struggling. Its underlying principle is that a stock's price is determined by its future earnings and dividends. And I'm about to show you exactly what to look for. If you follow the few simple strategies outlined below you'll find winners in no time and be on your way to becoming a real Buffett disciple.

The rules of long-term investment

Long-term investing is like any other investment style: you need a plan. Once you have the plan set up and a set of rules to follow, investing becomes easy. The reason most people fail in the stock market is not because they were 'unlucky' but rather that they didn't have a set of rules to follow. Think of it like following a recipe: if you add the right ingredients at the right time you have a pretty good chance of getting a tasty meal. Try to guess the ingredients and most of the time your meal will turn out to be a flop. It's the same with shares. Every successful investor, including Warren Buffett, follows a set of rules or strategies when choosing their investments.

Here are my simple rules for choosing companies with long-term potential. While it's rare for a company to fit every single rule (it would make things much easier if they did!), as long as it fits most of them you should still be looking at a pretty sound company.

- $ *Rule 1:* Is it a market leader (does it appear in the All Ords or the Dow Jones index)?

- $ *Rule 2:* Is its debt-to-equity ratio less than 75 per cent?

- $ *Rule 3:* Does it have a return on equity of 15 per cent or more?

- $ *Rule 4:* Will I get a five-year share return of 15 per cent or more?

- $ *Rule 5:* Is it a stable company (does it perform consistently year to year)?

- $ *Rule 6:* Is the current share price trading at less than 16 times the earnings per share price?

If it fits all of these rules, you might have just found yourself a bargain.

Rule 1: choose the market leaders

If looking at the share index page of your major newspaper overwhelms you, then the good news is that you're going to look only at the top companies in the top indices of your country; in other words, the All Ords if you're in Australia, the S&P 500 if you're in the US, or other top indices for you girls in other parts of the world—for example, FTSE 250 (UK) and S&P/TSX 60 (Canada).

Why no more than 500?

The stocks that fall into the All Ordinaries index (or any other world index) are considered the most prominent index for your stock exchange and these are the ones you'll often hear referred to in the news. While 500 (less for other major indices) may seem a lot to research, considering there are more than 1300 companies listed on the Australian Securities Exchange (and even more in other countries) it represents only the largest companies in terms of the market capitalisation of those listed, and probably the ones you've heard of rather than some little outback company that you have no idea about. You can get a list of all the companies that fall into this index from your stockbroker or on the ASX website.

You're going to concentrate only on these companies for two main reasons:

$ You want to buy the best companies for your money. If you stick with the market leaders you have a better chance of choosing nice, stable winners rather than erratic losers. You can further narrow down your selection to the top 200—or even the top 100—to start with if you're nervous about choosing the right leaders.

$ There's more information about these companies than the smaller ones. If you're going to make an informed decision,

61

you need as much background information as you can get. You need to know the company's past history, what it does and how much it makes. Often you can't get this information on smaller companies outside the top 500. Getting this information on the larger companies is relatively easy. Nearly all the information you want is available online or from your stockbroker.

The gist of the jargon

Market capitalisation: The value of a company; found by multiplying the number of shares available by the price of the shares.

While 500 may still seem an awful lot of stocks to choose from, you'll soon find it's not nearly as overwhelming as it sounds. Some online brokers even have advanced research functions where you can place all the criteria you're after into a search tool, and at the press of a button, the software does all the work for you.

Market leaders are usually the companies you already know about and see every day. They're the television stations you watch, the insurance companies you use and the food brands you eat. If you think about the larger companies in Australia that you know about, there's a very good chance they'll be in the top-500 companies listed on the stock exchange. Once you have your list of top-performing companies, you can start to narrow down your selection.

Oh, and if you want to find out which companies are included in the All Ords (or another index) you can usually find out by choosing the Market Indices section in your brokerage account and then clicking on the link or icon that will give you a list of all the companies in that index at the one time. You can even download this list so you can put it into a spreadsheet in a program such as Excel if you want to.

The lazy girl's guide to choosing market leaders

This part is pretty simple. Just decide that you're only going to choose market leaders—and that's that. The lazy work is done just by making a decision—it can't get easier than that!

Rule 2: keep debt down

Just as you wouldn't marry a guy who's in major debt, so too should you eliminate any company that's up to its eyeballs in borrowed money. However, that doesn't mean you should stick to only those companies that are debt free. Most companies do need to borrow some money to build and grow their company into a great empire while making you a lot of money along the way. There needs to be a balance, and you can easily find this out by looking at the company's debt-to-equity ratio.

The debt-to-equity ratio is a measure of the company's borrowings expressed as a percentage of shareholder equity. Banks and financial institutions don't need this figure as they're the ones who do the lending rather than the borrowing.

What you're looking for is a company whose debt-to-equity ratio is 75 per cent or less. You can find this figure under the risk section of your company data sheet. Figure 4.1 (overleaf) shows a copy of Wesfarmers Limited's key measures with the debt-to-equity ratio circled so you know where to look.

The reason for keeping debt to equity at or below this level is to avoid the companies that could turn into financial time bombs. If you were investing about 10 years ago, you could have avoided the financial collapses of HIH Insurance and One.Tel as their debt-to-equity ratios soared above 75 per cent, as did those of most dotcom companies during the dotcom debacle.

Figure 4.1: WES key measures showing debt-to-equity ratio

Company Profile	Last update: 29 April, 2011			
ASX Code: WES	Wesfarmers Limited			
Key Measures				
RISK	Company	All Ords	Sector 🔢	
Beta	0.70	1.06	0.71	
Current ratio	1.23	1.72	1.04	
Quick ratio	0.45	1.16	0.47	
Earnings stability	78.9%	55.4%	65.2%	
Debt/Equity ratio	27.0%	25.1%	24.1%	
Interest Cover	4.16	6.05	4.94	

Source: <www.CommSec.com.au>

While a high debt-to-equity ratio doesn't mean that a company is in trouble (often large companies such as shopping centres have high debt-to-equity ratios due to the number of properties they own and hence the number of property loans they have), it's still safer to stick to companies that fall below the 75 per cent mark. If your company does shut down, this figure means that there's still some money that the company can use towards paying out shareholders. If companies with debt-to-equity ratios above 100 per cent close down, there's no money left to pay out any costs they owe.

 Lazy girl's guide to finding the debt-to-equity ratio

Usually it's pretty easy to find the debt-to-equity ratio of any company that you're researching by entering the company code you want to research and then clicking the 'Research' button. The debt-to-equity ratio is usually listed in 'Key Measures' under 'Risk'.

Going through all those companies manually can take a bit of time. Nearly all online brokers have various search tools where you can enter search parameters to narrow down the field. If you're using CommSec as your online broker and want to find out the debt-to-equity ratio for all the companies listed on the stock exchange, you would log in to CommSec and go to the 'Advanced Search Tool' (which you will find under 'News & Research' > 'Company Research').

Then you can add the following into the search tool:

Category: Risk

Field: Debt-to-equity ratio

Option: Less than

Value: 0.75

Add Query

Run Query

When you run the query you're likely to get a large return of companies. However, most of these are probably not in the All Ords, so you'll need to decide whether this method is going to save you any time. If you want to be really lazy, buy a copy of Martin Roth's *Top Stocks*. A new edition of this title is published each year around October. It contains only those companies in the All Ords that fit certain financial criteria, including debt-to-equity ratios.

Rule 3: return on equity of at least 15 per cent

The next determinant is one of Buffett's fundamental rules and in my opinion the most important one. Return on equity (ROE) measures the amount of profit that a company has made on your behalf as a shareholder. In most cases this means the higher the profit, the higher the return on equity. Most investors would agree that return on equity is one of the most important measures of how a company is doing financially.

Return on equity is sometimes considered to be a good indicator of where the share price will go in the future. Buffett won't even look at a company unless its ROE is at least 15 per cent. If this rule is good enough for one of the richest men in the world, it's certainly good enough for us.

Take a look at some top Australian companies in table 4.1, and their return-on-equity figures.

Table 4.1: top Australian companies and their ROEs

Company	ROE %
AMP Limited	25.0
ANZ Bank	15.1
BHP Billiton	25.7
BXB—Brambles	27.6
CBA—Commonwealth Bank	16.8
CSL Limited	22.1
FGL—Fosters	26.5
NCM—Newcrest	15.1
TLS—Telstra	30.6
WOW—Woolworths	26.7

Figure 4.2 shows ANZ Bank's key measures, and where to find the ROE when looking at the company's financial information.

Rule 4: five-year share return of at least 15 per cent per annum

This rule is essentially broken up into two parts. The first part is simply that the company has to be listed on the stock exchange for at least five years. This means that new floats and initial public offerings (IPOs) don't qualify. The reason for this is that companies listed for fewer than five years usually don't have enough information available to enable you to objectively analyse their figures.

Five years is also the approximate time period for which a long-term investor (as opposed to a short-term player) will hold an investment.

Figure 4.2: ANZ's 15.1 per cent ROE for September 2010

Company Profile	Last update: 29 April, 2011						New Search		

ASX Code: **ANZ**   **Australia & New Zealand Banking Group Ltd**

Main View | Forecasts | Financials | Company Info | News | Announcements | Analysis |
Dividends | Shareholders | Directors

Buy | Sell | Depth | Chart | Watchlist

Company Historicals

HISTORICAL FINANCIALS

	9/01	9/02	9/03	9/04	9/05	9/06	9/07	9/08	9/09	9/10
Net profit before abnormals ($million)	1,751	2,051	2,246	2,633	2,972	3,560	3,887	2,983	3,739	5,025
Net profit ($million)	1,751	2,205	2,246	2,717	2,934	3,661	4,143	3,273	2,910	4,501
Income tax rate(%)	32.7	27.9	28.3	29.3	29.0	29.2	28.6	26.3	32.8	31.8
Employees (thousands)	22.5	22.5	23.1	28.8	31.0	32.3	34.4	36.9	37.7	46.9
Shareholders equity ($million)	9,012	10,073	11,558	16,920	17,603	19,001	21,139	25,619	31,493	33,220
Return on equity(%)	19.4	20.4	19.4	15.6	16.9	18.7	18.4	11.6	11.9	(15.1)
Payout ratio(%)	63	62	64	70	69	66	66	92	61	65

Source: <www.CommSec.com.au>

Long-term investors are willing to ride out the day-to-day market fluctuations for long-term gains. They don't have to watch the market every day; in fact, you really only need to check it once or twice a year to see whether the financials are still on track.

The second part of this rule is that the company should have returned an average of 15 per cent per annum over the past five years. Any psychologist will tell you that the best indicator of future behaviour is past behaviour. You want to know that your company has performed well in the past so that you can be confident that it might also perform well in the future. The rule also measures a degree of predictability. And, if you're investing for the long term, you want some indication that your choices and decisions are based on fact, rather than gut feeling. This is not to say that every share that has been profitable in the past will be so in the future. There are many duds that have shown amazing growth only to fall off the cliff the very next year. However, if you combine many of my rules mentioned so far (return on equity, low debt), you can be reasonably confident you have a real winner.

The gist of the jargon

Initial public offerings (IPOs): Also called 'floats'. When a new company is about to be listed on the ASX, potential shareholders may be able to buy into the company before it's actually listed by filling out some paperwork. Once the company goes public the applicant owns shares in this newly listed company. This is how most people bought into Telstra when it first listed.

This rule is a bit tougher than the others, especially right now as we've just had a major market crash and the stock price is only just recovering. In fact, if you'd looked at the Average Annual Shareholder Return for the past five years two years ago, you'd have seen that practically all companies showed a negative return. Even today, most companies are only showing a small return—usually less than 15 per cent.

Some companies don't always make a consistent gain of exactly 15 per cent year in and year out (it would be nice if they did). Sometimes stocks may make only 3 or 4 per cent in one year and then go on to make an outstanding 26 per cent the following year. Sometimes they might even decrease a few per cent over one year. What's more important is what a company does over the long term—this is what you're most interested in.

While I try to choose stocks that make more than an average 15 per cent per year, I'm certainly not going to reject a stock if it made only 8 per cent and the rest of its fundamentals are outstanding. Over the long run, as long as a stock is consistently making good profits, it should definitely be considered.

So, while I like to get a five-year return of 15 per cent or more, this rule is not essential, especially as the rules for choosing a great company can be flawed when there's been a market crash. It doesn't mean that the company is bad overall; just that investors got scared of the whole market and jumped ship like it was on fire.

Take the example of Woolworths shown in figure 4.3. Over the long term, this stock has returned a healthy profit to its shareholders (15.9 per cent per annum over 10 years and even a healthy 11.5 per cent per annum over five years). If you followed this rule too literally you could overlook Woolworths because the five-year return isn't quite 15 per cent. In fact, the three-year return shows only a modest gain of 1.1 per cent. Would you reject this stock on those results? I certainly wouldn't.

Figure 4.3: WOW annual shareholder return

Company Profile   Last update: 21 February, 2011

ASX Code: WOW   Woolworths Limited

Total Shareholder Return
(avg annual rate)

1yr	3yr	5yr	10yr
4.0%	1.1%	11.5%	15.9%

Source: <www.CommSec.com.au>

Since you're holding for the long term and you know there's just been a market fall, you can still feel confident holding shares like these knowing that, over the long term, the company will probably be okay.

Finding a company's shareholder return

While online brokers have different layouts, generally you'll find the average annual rates on the main view of the company research page.

Rule 5: nice and stable wins the race

My last rule for selecting the companies I'm interested in is earnings stability. Again, you want your companies to be very stable in their earnings growth. Nice, stable companies are much easier to predict than volatile, bad ones.

I like to make sure the stocks I choose have at least 80 per cent earnings stability. The reason for this is that the more stable a company is year in year out, the easier it is to be confident it will continue to be so in the future.

Earnings stability is a measure of the stability of the growth of earnings from year to year expressed as a percentage. The maximum figure of 100 per cent represents earnings that go up (or down) by the same percentage each year. A low percentage means the company's earnings are more volatile and vary significantly from year to year. A good high earnings stability figure is also usually indicative of a good and capable management team being in place.

I wouldn't use earnings stability on its own as a determinant of which stock to buy; a company could be consistently losing money by the same amount each year and have a high earnings stability figure (hey, at least it's consistent!). But if the rest of its fundamentals are on track, I'll definitely consider it. I like my long-term investment stocks to be nice and predictable—some would even say boring—doing the same thing year in year out.

Earnings stability is one of the factors (after return on equity) that I consider to be the most important. While occasionally I'll choose a company with slightly lower than 80 per cent stability if the rest of its fundamentals look good, I'll never go much lower. And, while these stocks might be more predictable and safer, believe me there's nothing boring about owning a company that consistently makes money!

Figure 4.4 shows earnings stability in the risk section of key measures for Woolworths.

Figure 4.4: finding a company's earnings stability

Company Profile   Last update: 29 April, 2011

ASX Code: WOW   Woolworths Limited

Key Measures

RISK	Company	All Ords	Sector
Beta	0.71	1.06	0.71
Current ratio	0.73	1.72	1.04
Quick ratio	0.20	1.16	0.47
Earnings stability	87.9%	55.4%	65.2%
Debt/Equity ratio	46.8%	25.1%	24.1%
Interest Cover	12.99	6.05	4.94

Source: <www.CommSec.com.au>

You'll generally find the earnings stability on the main view of the company research page under the risk heading.

 Lazy girl's guide to which 'rules' are most important

It's very rare to find a company that fits all these rules exactly, especially—as I've already mentioned—if the market has gone through turbulent times, meaning returns are all over the place.

I thought I'd put the first five rules in order of importance so that you know which ones should be absolutely adhered to, and which ones can show a little wiggle room.

$ *Market leaders*. They must be in the top 500, or at least the top 100 (if I don't feel like looking at a lot of companies), before I'll even look at them.

$ *Low debt-to-equity ratio (or at least below 75 per cent)*. Think about what business the company does, though, before you consider this rule. Banks have no debt-to-equity ratio because they do the lending. Property groups will probably have a high debt-to-equity ratio since they borrow lots of money for developing buildings.

$ *ROE at least 15 per cent*. That's my next most important rule and one that I'd never waiver on no matter what the market conditions are.

$ *Earnings stability 80 per cent or higher*. I like a nice, stable company—not too many surprises, thanks very much.

$ *The five-year share price*. Finally, the rule that gives you some room to breathe. In an ideal world the long-term share price would be above 15 per cent and when the market is operating normally you'll see this more often. However, in rough market conditions this could be lower, so have a look at the 10-year and one-year returns to see whether you're comfortable with how the company handled the crisis.

Rule 6: the price you pay

By now you've probably narrowed down your list to the top 10 or 20 stocks that you're interested in, so it's time to buy—right? Hang on, not so fast! You're not going to just pay the price that's offered in the market! Oh no, you need to wait until the price is right. You want a bargain for your money, not an overpriced asset.

You want to wait until the stock goes on sale. Yes, stocks do go on sale occasionally — it's called a downturn in the market, and while some people get upset when the share prices go down, I look at it as an opportunity to buy into those companies that I've always wanted at a bargain price.

So what's your ideal target price?

Buying stocks below their true or intrinsic value is what a lot of investors like — to snag a bargain. They expect that once the market acknowledges a company as a winner the price of its shares will increase accordingly. Some value investors will buy into a company just because it's cheap; however, under my rules you need to first find a great company before you even look at the price. It's one thing to buy into a company because it's cheap; it's another thing to buy into a cheap company!

Usually the maximum price I'm prepared to pay is 16 times earnings. I'll simply look for the earnings per share (EPS) figure on the company's financial information sheet and multiply that figure by 16 to find the price I'm prepared to pay for the share. The EPS can be found listed in the newspaper near the share price or on the company information sheet. Figure 4.5 (overleaf) shows that QBE Insurance Group's EPS for the year 2011 is 170.2 and that its dividend is 129 cents per share.

In the QBE example, EPS is 170.2. You multiply this figure by 16: $170.2 \times 16 = \$27.23$. So $27.23 is the maximum price you would pay for this stock. (At the time of writing, QBE's share price was trading at $18.66, which is lower than our target price — therefore QBE represents good value.)

Let's look at another company: FGL (Fosters). Right now FGL's EPS is 35.7. Multiplied by 16, you get a price of $5.71. At the time of writing, FGL was trading at just about this price, so it represents excellent value.

Many people use this method to find 'cheap' shares hoping that they'll rise in price soon afterwards when the market realises that they're undervalued. While this can sometimes be the case, I wouldn't be in too much of a hurry to buy cheap companies unless the rest of their fundamentals are sound. Sometimes cheap shares are cheap for a reason.

Often, a few companies on your target list might already be at the price you're willing to pay, and you can buy these now if you like. However, you'll have to keep an eye on the rest until they drop to your target of 16 times earnings.

Figure 4.5: QBE's EPS for the year 2011

Company Profile   Last update: 21 February, 2011

ASX Code: **QBE**   **QBE Insurance Group Limited**

Main View | Forecasts | Financials | Company Info | News
Dividends | Shareholders | Directors

Earnings and Dividends
Forecast (cents per share)

	2009	2010	2011	2012
EPS	192.8	125.2	170.2	163.1
DPS	128.0	125.0	129.0	130.2

Source: <www.CommSec.com.au>

How set in stone is this rule?

It's true that often you'll have a hard time trying to find a stock that's 'cheap' enough to buy. That's when market crashes are your friend because suddenly everything you wanted to buy previously, but couldn't, falls low enough in price for you to buy. It's sale time!

However, sometimes you just want to get into the market.

If you can't choose between a number of companies, none of which is trading at or below its 'EPS × 16' price, pick those that are the closest to this price and study the high and low prices they've shown over the past few months.

If, over the past few months, one of these companies dipped to a price you're prepared to pay, I'd suggest waiting because it's likely to dip back to the price again. However, if it seems to be on a steady upward trend, perhaps you could be a bit lenient and go for it now.

 ### Lazy girl's research into long-term investing

I usually like to put the top 500 shares in an Excel spreadsheet with nine columns. Column 1 has the company code in it; column 2 the ROE; column 3 the earnings stability; column 4 the five-year percentage; column 5 the debt-to-equity ratio; column 6 the EPS; column 7 the EPS × 16; column 8 the current price (I only fill this one in if I'm interested in buying it); and column 9 indicates whether the share is currently trading below 16 × EPS (either with a yes or no).

Finding this information is pretty simple if you have an online broker. It's just a matter of putting the code into the 'Get quote' box and then clicking on 'Research'. Once you know where to look to find all of the figures it shouldn't take you more than one minute per company to put them into your Excel spreadsheet. Five hundred companies at one minute each equals 500 minutes or eight hours (it usually takes me *way* less time than this, though).

If you don't want to do all 500, then just do 200 or even the top 100 shares (ASX 100).

The company financials are updated twice a year (usually around March and September) so you will need to keep your spreadsheet up to date.

To get you started, I've done the research for you on the top 20 companies (minus the last two columns) in table 4.2.

Table 4.2: the ASX 20

ASX Top 20	ROE	Earnings stab	5-year percentage	Debt/Eq	EPS	EPS × 16
AMP	25.0%	57.4%	−1.2%	n/a	40.5	$6.48
ANZ	15.1%	58.3%	4.8%	n/a	215.0	$34.40
BHP	25.7%	56.7%	16.1%	32.5%	392.0	$62.72
BXB	27.6%	79.3%	−3.2%	116.1%	35.0	$5.60
CBA	16.8%	81.5%	9.7%	n/a	412.4	$65.98
CSL	22.1%	54.2%	17.5%	11.0%	177.6	$28.42
FGL	26.5%	65.1%	6.4%	95.0%	35.7	$5.71
MQG	9.4%	51.4%	−5.1%	n/a	272.4	$43.58
NAB	11.9%	76.1%	−1.0%	n/a	240.0	$38.40
NCM	15.1%	35.3%	15.6%	8.6%	162.7	$26.03
ORG	5.6%	61.1%	22.7%	34.0%	74.8	$11.97
QBE	19.3%	49.8%	3.2%	n/a	170.2	$27.23
RIO	24.0%	44.8%	10.6%	24.6%	1003.1	$160.50
TLS	30.6%	76.7%	1.5%	117.4%	24.1	$3.86
WBC	15.4%	55.9%	6.2%	n/a	208.0	$33.28
WDC	10.6%	No Info	−0.3%	n/a	69.1	$11.06
WES	6.3%	78.8%	5.7%	27.0%	189.4	$30.30
WOW	26.7%	87.9%	11.5%	46.8%	176.5	$28.24
WPL	12.8%	45.6%	3.6%	44.3%	177.3	$28.37
WRT	No Info					

Do you see any winners in this list? From a quick look I'd personally be interested in CBA (Commonwealth Bank) and WOW (Woolworths) because they each have a good ROE and earnings stability. In addition, they're trading at below 16 × EPS so they're at a good price.

I may also list the top 100 shares (or perhaps even the top 200) with all their statistics and put them on my website at <www.shoppingforshares.com> so you can all see at a glance some good investment choices. Let's see how lazy I get as to whether I actually do this. Thinking about helping you out counts, though — right?

Dividends

You've chosen your stocks, and they're giving a healthy return on your dollar year by year: can it get any better? Yes, it can, because twice a year most companies will send you a nice little cheque, simply for owning their shares. Dividends are paid to shareholders from the company's net profit; therefore, if the company is doing well, it will typically pay a higher dividend.

Dividends are expressed as cents per share. In figure 4.5 (on p. 74), QBE paid 129 cents per share for the year 2011. If you held 500 shares that would mean you probably received dividends to the value of $645 for the year, simply for owning them! Not bad for a bit of pocket money.

Some investors use the strategy of holding shares simply for the income they can give. Obviously, some stocks pay much higher dividends than others. Property trusts are known to be among the highest payers of dividends per share (often referred to as dividend yield). With these types of companies, while the share price doesn't increase much year to year, with dividend yields usually better than 7 per cent they represent a much better place for your money than an ordinary old bank account. If you're interested in high-yield companies, see the section at the end of this chapter.

Not all companies pay dividends, however, and there's no requirement for them to do so. Sometimes a company may decide that it's in its best interests to reinvest its earnings back into the business instead. That's not necessarily a bad thing and can sometimes be quite good for company growth. So, whether a company pays dividends or not should not be a basis for your decision to buy for the long term; it's just a nice little bonus if they do.

Franked / fully franked

In most of the larger companies listed on the stock exchange, the tax on dividends is usually already paid for you. If the dividend is listed as fully franked, or 100 per cent franked, it means the company has already paid the tax on that share at the company rate. What that means for you is that, when it comes around to tax time, depending on your own tax rate, you might get the dividend tax free, or even receive a tax credit, which can be used to offset tax on your other income. Your accountant will be able to give you further advice on this.

Don't be too concerned if the company you've chosen doesn't pay fully franked dividends. Many people will ignore a company simply because it doesn't pay a fully franked dividend; however, to do so would be to miss out on a whole stack of great companies. While it's good if the company does pay fully franked dividends, don't discount a company simply because it doesn't. Your ultimate goal is to choose a company because of the likelihood of its price rising—whether it saves you a bit of tax from the dividends is really a non-issue in my opinion.

Share-price behaviour for dividends

Often when a stock approaches the ex-dividend date the share price and volume of activity (the buying and selling) increases quite quickly. Once the stock hits its ex-dividend date, the price drops off again. Long-term investors need not be too concerned with these fluctuations, but short-term players can take advantage of this (see the rules for short-term investing in chapter 5).

The gist of the jargon

Ex dividend: The date a company sets for when all shareholders holding shares will receive the company dividend. You must be holding the shares prior to the ex-dividend date. If you sell shares prior to this date, you will not receive the dividend. If you sell shares after this date, you will still be entitled to receive the dividend.

It's interesting to note that you don't necessarily have to hold shares for a full 12 months to get the full dividend. You could easily buy the day before the required date, and then sell when the stock goes ex dividend. In this instance, you could get six months' worth of dividends simply for holding the shares for two or three days (assuming the company pays dividends twice a year).

However, doing this will usually mean that you're buying at a high price and then selling lower so you need to factor this in before you go looking for companies that are about to pay out dividends.

Buying for income — listed property trusts and other high-yield companies

Most of this chapter so far has been focused on buying shares that increase in price, often called buying for capital growth. But a section on dividends wouldn't be complete without talking about another investment strategy and that's buying for income. As I've mentioned, companies generally pay dividends twice a year, and most dividend yields range from about 1 to 5 per cent per annum, the average being 4 per cent per annum.

However, there are a number of companies that offer dividend yields much higher than this. Listed property trusts are probably the most common of these, with their yields reaching levels of 8 to 10 per cent, sometimes even more. Imagine a bank account paying that sort of interest! While these sorts of trusts rarely make great gains in capital growth, the income they provide can be a nice little earner in your long-term investment portfolio.

Buying into a property trust is a bit different from buying into a regular company. Instead of buying into one company, as the name suggests you're buying into an already professionally managed portfolio of real estate. So, essentially, you could be a real-estate investor owning many properties with only a tiny portion of your own money!

The dividends are derived from rental income generated from the properties held in the trust — industrial, office, retail, hotel real estate or a combination of all of these types of property. The price of these stocks doesn't seem to move as much as regular investments so, since the volatility of these types of investment is usually fairly low, they're generally considered more stable or less risky than regular stocks.

Have a look at figure 4.6, which shows the company profile for IHF — ING Real Estate Healthcare Fund. As you can see, IHF has a high dividend yield of 9.1 per cent (and because its dividend stability is more than 97 per cent, you can be confident it will probably pay the same amount nearly every year). This is much higher than the average market dividend yield of only 6.2 per cent. It's a fairly new property group — it's only been around for slightly more than three years — but if you held this stock you would have gained a modest 5.5 per cent increase in share value over those three years. More important would be the consistent

9.1 per cent dividend returns that you received each year—a nice steady income for your money.

Figure 4.6: IHF's dividend yield of 9.1 per cent

Company Profile   Last update: 29 April, 2011

ASX Code: IHF   ING Real Estate Healthcare Fund

Key Measures

VALUE	Company	All Ords	Sector
P/E ratio	9.28	11.03	11.92
P/B ratio	0.85	1.42	0.76
P/E Growth ratio	--	0.94	1.81

INCOME	Company	All Ords	Sector
Dividend yield	9.1%	5.0%	6.2%
Franking	0.0%		
Tax adjusted dividend yield	5.0%	3.8%	3.5%
Dividend stability	97.6%	0.0%	93.5%

Source: <www.CommSec.com.au>

Let's look at another example using a company that's been around at bit longer.

HHY (Hastings High Yield Fund) has an average annual return of 6.2 per cent but, more importantly, it has produced a dividend yield of 12.2 per cent (with more than 95 per cent stability).

If the dividend yield was the same for the past five years (and it probably was with such a high dividend stability figure), and you'd bought 10 000 HHY shares five years ago, your dividend return alone would be $1220 per annum over five years, or $6100. Add the fact that your share price has also increased by 6.2 per cent and you're looking at some pretty serious returns.

If you're interested in trying this method of investing, you can find a list of property trusts in the S&P/ASX 200 Property Trusts sector on the ASX website, or ask your broker. Alternatively you could do a search for only those companies with high dividend yields. As you're investing for the long term, it's important that you still look at other factors such as company stability and debt ratios before using this method but, if the company seems a good risk, by all means go ahead and enjoy those cheques!

$ $ $

The most successful investors the world over use a buy-and-hold strategy when it comes to the sharemarket. Even if you're determined to be a short-term player (using the strategies in the next chapter), I'd recommend that you hold some stocks in nice, safe, long-term investment companies using some of the strategics outlined here as well, just to keep your portfolio balanced.

Long-term investing is like buying a classic diamond ring. Over the long term it should provide you with happiness every time you look at it. And as the diamond should increase in value over time, so should your shares. Shares are the new 'girl's best friend'.

Investing for the short term

Chapter 5

Sell! Buy! Ever wanted to scream those words down the phone to your broker? Ever wanted to boast at a dinner party about how a certain stock just increased 20 per cent in price overnight and you managed to spot the trend early and take advantage of it? While this might sound a bit Hollywood, when it comes to short-term investing it can be possible to take advantage of quick movements in the market if you know what to look for.

Short-term investing—or trading, as some like to call it—involves taking advantage of short-term moves in the market and (hopefully) making a quick profit. There are many strategies to employ for short-term investing, but most involve looking at charts, following economic trends or taking advantage of certain company situations such as takeovers or announcements of improved profits.

Short-term investors might hold a share for one year, one month or even one day, if they're so inclined. Some investors even trade by the hour (day traders), although I've never been brave enough to try this strategy. My preferred time line for holding short-term investments is usually about two months, but this varies from company to company. The shortest time I've held shares in a company is three days, after which the price increased to the level that I was aiming for (I was doing a happy dance that day—it was a huge rise in a short space of time), and so I sold this stock and cashed in my profit. While I knew that this share was doing well and I expected it to increase in the future, no doubt a little bit of luck was involved for its price to increase so quickly in such a short period of time.

You need to decide how long you're going to hold a share before you buy it so that you can plan at what price you're going to sell.

Once you have a plan in place, investing becomes like following a recipe and you'll find it much easier to make decisions. Just as with long-term investing, short-term investing follows a set of rules for choosing the companies to invest in. This chapter will help you narrow down your selections so you too can become proficient in using the methods that have worked for me.

Trading can be fun

Watching the market, especially when your own money is involved, can be exceptionally exciting. Emotions can range from ecstatic highs when your share's price rises to depressing lows when it falls.

But if you're careful and you keep a level head, trading can be just plain fun. I enjoy the thrill of watching my shares move and dance and twirl. Sometimes I get giddy watching how fast some share prices move, and disappointed when they don't move fast enough.

Short-term investing is definitely more of an emotional roller-coaster than long-term investing, but if you're attracted to that sort of excitement, then maybe you'll find it fun too.

Whether I make more money from investing short term or long term is really not an issue for me. Sometimes I do make more money from short-term investing; other times long-term investing wins out. The debate over which investment strategy is better has been raging for nearly as long as the market has been open and I'm sure you'll find just as many people telling you one way is better as the other. I like both methods: I like long-term investing for the security I feel from those shares, but boy I like the day-to-day play of watching my shares wiggle as well. Both methods have made me money; both methods can work. I just find short-term investment more fun.

But you have to do a bit of homework first. When it comes to short-term investing, that homework is usually called technical analysis.

What is technical analysis?

Whereas fundamental analysis is analysing a company's worth by looking at its financial background, technical analysis involves primarily looking at the price and volume history of a share.

You don't take into consideration what the company does or how much profit it makes; you only check whether the share is increasing in price and volume. Technical analysis is basically just following the trend of what the share is already doing. If it's consistently increasing in price it's probably a buy and if it's consistently decreasing in price it's probably a sell.

If you've ever looked at a stock chart, the two main sets of information shown are usually the price and the volume over a set period of time.

The volume (how many shares were bought or sold) is usually shown at the bottom in a column format, and the price is usually plotted into a line or bar graph at the top. Let's have a look at the chart in figure 5.1 in more detail.

Figure 5.1 shows a simple line graph for ASX for a six-month period. This chart plots the closing price each day and lines are drawn between points to show the share's price as a wiggly line. The bottom section shows the volume (how many shares were bought and sold that day) in millions. Both sections can give us a lot of information. Firstly, we can see at a glance in which general direction the share is moving and, secondly, we can see whether there's been any unusual trading activity in the share (volume that is much higher than the usual volume). This chart shows high volume at the end of October, which corresponds to a high spike in price. I'll take a guess and say that the share probably paid out shares to those holding them from late October and went ex dividend at the bottom of the spike. The only other high-volume trading days correspond to increases in price, so it's safe to assume that this company's price movement is bullish for this time period.

Charting is one of the short-term player's best friends, because it gives a quick visual clue as to what a share's price is doing. It involves watching for specific movements on a chart to assess what the share is likely to do next. The most useful charts are usually the bar chart or the candlestick chart (figures 5.2 on p. 89 and 5.3 on p. 91 respectively).

These charts are similar to the line chart except that they show more information. Instead of just plotting the closing price, these charts show four prices for each point: the open and closing price as well as the high and low price for the period shown (usually daily, weekly or monthly, but it can be for shorter or longer terms).

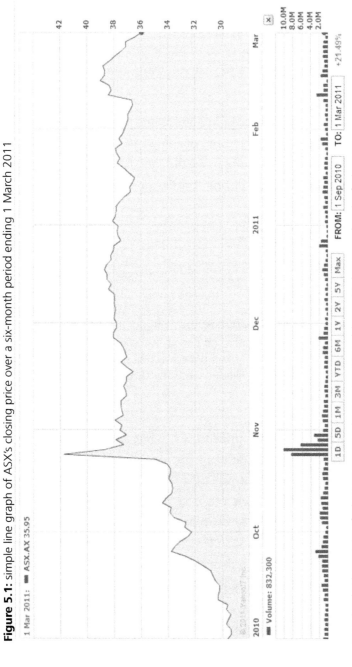

Figure 5.1: simple line graph of ASX's closing price over a six-month period ending 1 March 2011

Figure 5.2 is a bar-chart version of figure 5.1, while figure 5.3 on p. 91 is a candlestick version. Compare the differences and decide which one you like best. More information is displayed in these figures than in figure 5.1 so that you can gain more insight into the share's behaviour.

In figure 5.2 ASX's price points are shown by a small tick on the left of the line representing the opening price. The small tick on the right is the closing price, and the line itself represents all the prices that the share hit during that day or period.

The gist of the jargon

Candlestick chart: A technical analysis chart that shows the price of a share for each period as a box (or candle) shape with vertical lines to the top and bottom. The top and bottom of the box represent the opening and closing price of the share and the lines above and below the boxes represent the high and low prices that the share reached for the specified period. If the box (or candlestick) is blank (or green) the closing price was higher than the opening price and if the box is filled (or red) the closing price was lower than the opening price.

The candlestick chart presents the same information as the bar chart in a slightly different format. The thick body of the candlestick indicates the opening and closing prices, whereas the line protruding from the body is all the prices the share reached for that day above or below the opening and closing prices. If the body of the candlestick is blank (or green), then the closing price was higher than the opening price, representing a bullish day. If the candlestick is filled (or red) the closing price finished lower and it was a bearish day. The taller the candle, the bigger the difference between the price points for that day.

Figure 5.2: bar chart of ASX's six-month share price

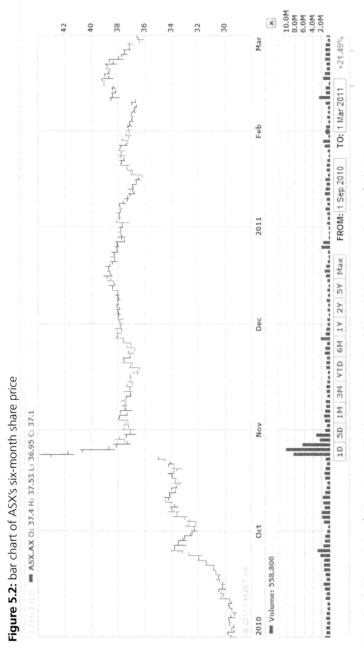

The gist of the jargon

Bar chart: A technical analysis chart that lists the opening price of a share shown as a small vertical line with a tick on the left for each period. The closing price is shown as a tick on the right, with the body of the line representing all the prices the share reached for that period.

I prefer candlestick charts because I can see the number of blank and filled candles for that company and quickly decide whether the share price movement is bullish or bearish. If there are many filled candles the share is probably one to avoid or sell, but if there are many blank candles, it could be a good buy.

The gist of the jargon

Uptrend: When a share is moving in an upward pattern. Drawing a trendline on a chart can confirm this.

Downtrend: When a share is moving in a downward pattern.

Reading charts and following trends

Pick up any book on charting and you'll start to hear strange terminology such as 'spinning top' and 'hanging man combined with Bollinger bands' to describe certain chart patterns. Sometimes all these different chart interpretations can seem overwhelming.

When I first started charting I was determined to find the Holy Grail pattern that would provide unlimited profit potential but, alas, I never found it. In fact, the more complicated I made things on my charts the harder it became for me to actually choose anything at all, so I scaled it back down to looking at just a few things—nice and simple.

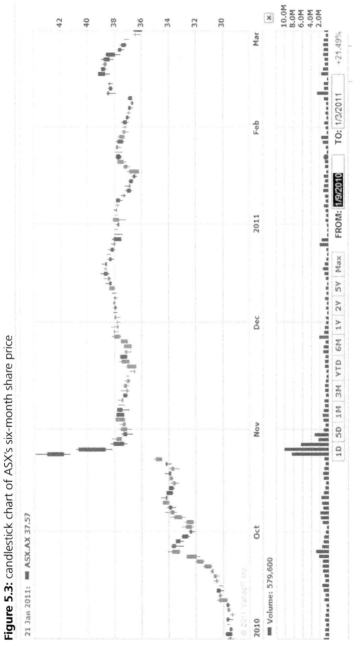

Figure 5.3: candlestick chart of ASX's six-month share price

Reproduced with permission of Yahoo! Inc. © 2011 Yahoo! Inc. YAHOO! and the YAHOO! logo are trademarks of Yahoo! Inc.

While interpreting every chart movement might be helpful to some, I found it was better when I just used a few and stuck to them. The simpler I made the charts, the simpler it was to work out what to buy.

So what do you need to look for? You should be looking at the overall trend of a share by looking at the chart and trying to determine the direction of price movement. First, I draw a trendline on the chart. Second, I look at the moving average of the share's price, which determines whether the trend is slowing down or speeding up. Let's look at these two tools further.

Drawing a trendline — where is the share going?

A share can be going only one of three ways: up, down or sideways. Uptrends and downtrends are the easiest to spot and a trendline can be drawn to confirm your observations. The hardest trend to determine (and unfortunately the most common) is the sideways trend because you always seem to be trying to figure out whether it's about to break out and go up or down.

When drawing trendlines, try to pick three or four clear price points that hit the line. While you can draw your lines from either the bottom or the top of the price points, I prefer to use the top of the price points for downtrends and the bottom of the price points for uptrends because you can clearly see whether a new price point is breaking through this line, which would indicate a change in the direction of the share price.

The chart in figure 5.4 shows two distinct trendlines for Leighton Holdings (LEI) over the past 12 months. You can see two clear trendlines: the first one decreasing and the second one increasing.

Figure 5.4: LEI chart showing two distinct trendlines—the first a downtrend line and the second an uptrend line
LEIGHTON HOLDINGS FPO

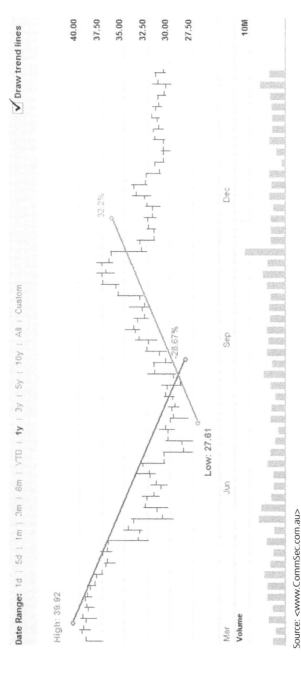

Source: <www.CommSec.com.au>

By drawing a line that hits the tops of the bar chart share prices you can see that there was a breakout around August 2010 where the prices started to increase above the trendline. The stock then went into an uptrend for two or three months until it fell through the line again in November, starting a sideways trend.

In this case, you might have seen the signs and purchased LEI in August for approximately $30 per share and then, because your share broke through your uptrend line in November, sold at approximately $35 per share, making a quick 16 per cent return in just three months.

A sideways trend is probably the most common trend you'll see, and it can be difficult for short-term investing because you usually have no clues as to where the price is going to go next.

It can often be helpful to draw lines along the top and bottom of a sideways band. This way you can see whether the price breaks through and deserves more attention or not. From figure 5.5, are you able to predict where the price of Orica Limited (ORI) is going? I haven't a clue, until it breaks out of its sideways band. I usually avoid a share in a sideways band until I'm sure of the direction it's going in.

Moving averages — simple or exponential?

A moving average looks like a wavy line on the chart running close to the share prices. It takes the sum of the closing prices over a determined period of time and averages them out into a simple line graph that's overlaid on a regular chart. You can use any time period you like — five days, 20 weeks — it's entirely up to you, although I usually stick with 15- or 30-day moving averages. You can even use two or more moving averages of different time periods on the same chart if you like.

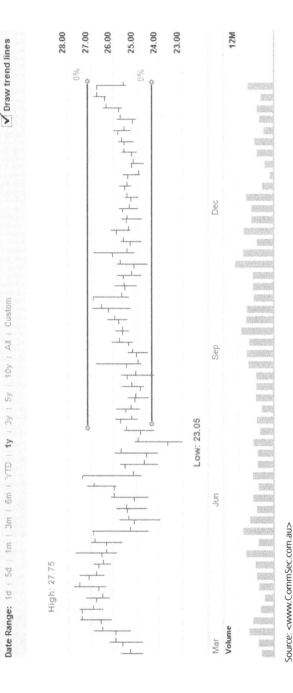

Figure 5.5: ORI chart showing a clear sideways band

ORICA LIMITED FPO

Date Range: 1d | 5d | 1m | 3m | 6m | YTD | **1y** | 3y | 5y | 10y | All | Custom

✓ Draw trend lines

High: 27.75

Low: 23.05

Mar   Jun   Sep   Dec

Volume   12M

Source: <www.CommSec.com.au>

There are two main types of moving average: the simple moving average and the exponential moving average. Whereas a simple moving average gives each price equal weight over the given time period, the exponential moving average gives more weight to the most recent prices. Moving averages are most useful for determining whether a trend is slowing down or speeding up because you can see at a glance whether the peaks and falls of the moving average line are increasing or decreasing in pitch. You can also see whether the share is trending up or down as all prices above the moving average line are generally bullish, and all those below are usually bearish.

The gist of the jargon

Simple moving average (SMA): A line that can be displayed on a company's chart to show the average share price of that company over a certain time period (usually the past 15 or 30 days—but you can enter any time period you like). By choosing to display the SMA on your chart you can see whether the current price is above or below the average price for that share.

Exponential moving average (EMA): Similar to the SMA in that it averages out the share price over a required time period, but it places more emphasis on recent prices so that your moving average is weighted closer to current share price movements.

Figure 5.6 shows a 20-day exponential moving average (EMA) and a 50-day EMA for Qantas Airways Limited (QAN). There are several interesting movements to notice in this chart.

In mid November the price dropped through both EMAs (which is a very bearish sign) and then, not long afterwards, in late November the two EMAs crossed and the 20-day EMA became lower than the 50-day EMA.

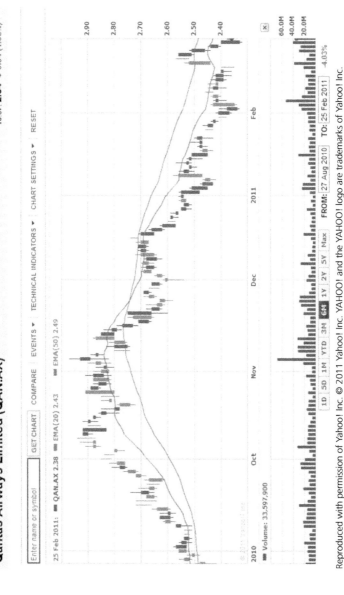

Figure 5.6: QAN chart showing a 20-day EMA crossing through a 50-day EMA in November 2010

Qantas Airways Limited (QAN.AX)

Reproduced with permission of Yahoo! Inc. © 2011 Yahoo! Inc. YAHOO! and the YAHOO! logo are trademarks of Yahoo! Inc.

A crossing of two moving averages is usually significant as it represents a strong trend. If the shorter term moving average crosses below the longer term moving average, this is called a 'dead cross'. This indicates that the stock has entered a strong downtrend and, if you own some of that stock, it might be time to jump ship before you lose too much money. If, however, the opposite is the case and the shorter term moving average crosses above the longer term moving average, this is called a 'golden cross' and may indicate that the share is now moving into an uptrend. But you will need to look at other signs in the chart to confirm this before you decide to buy.

Commonwealth Bank's chart (see figure 5.7) shows both a dead cross in its downtrend and a golden cross in its uptrend. If you could spot the trends earlier, CBA's chart would show many positive indications.

I find that the crossing of moving averages usually comes after the price has already changed direction, so it's useful to me only in that it confirms a trend rather than helping me choose a share to buy. There are plenty of other patterns you can apply to charts to help determine the direction; however, I don't find them any more helpful than the basics. If you can't tell the direction of a share from trendlines or moving averages (or even just by looking at the share), it probably isn't worth further investigation. Find a stock that's easier to determine.

The gist of the jargon

Golden cross: When a shorter term moving average crosses up above a longer term moving average. Considered very bullish.

Dead cross: When a shorter term moving average crosses down below a longer term moving average. Considered very bearish.

Figure 5.7: CBA showing a dead cross at October 2010 and a golden cross at December 2010

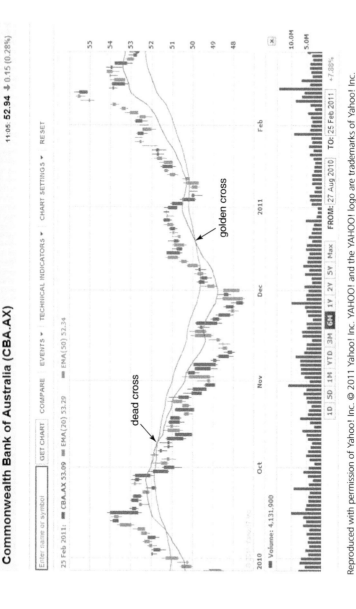

The rules of short-term investment

As with any investment style you need some rules to follow so that investing becomes easier. As with long-term investing, following these rules should increase your chances of being successful in the market. Having a plan is probably even more important in short-term investing because the market can move quickly and you want your rules, not your emotions, to guide you in tricky situations.

When I first started to dabble in short-term investing, I thought it was a brilliant concept for choosing really cheap stocks; after all, they only had to go up one cent and I'd have made a fortune. I promptly bought a stock that was priced at 0.08 cents. I thought if it increased just 0.01 cent I'd make a nice little profit. I bought $2000 worth, which equated to approximately 25 000 shares. I thought that if it went up even 0.01 cent I'd make a quick $125. Wow, imagine if it went up 0.02 cents!

Example

Share price: 0.08 × 25 000 = $2000
Share aim: 0.09 × 25 000 = $2250 (profit: $250)
Share dream: 0.10 × 25 000 = $2500 (profit: $500)

I sat back and waited, and waited, and waited. I hadn't really done my homework; this was a stock that was very illiquid (not very much trading activity). After about a month I realised that nothing was happening with this share and I wanted to get rid of it. That's not as easy as it sounds with a share that doesn't have much volume. No-one seemed to want to buy at 0.08 cents; in fact, nobody wanted to buy at 0.07 cents either. I ended up having to sell at a loss at 0.06 cents.

My dream of a quick profit was soon shattered. I lost $500, which was 25 per cent less than what I'd started with. Take my advice:

all those really cheap stocks might be cheap for a reason; do your research before investing in any of the 'penny stocks'. This was a lesson learnt—if I wanted to make some money through short-term investing, I needed a plan!

Nowadays, while I might give myself some room to move when choosing long-term investments, I'm much stricter about following a plan with my short-term investments. The steps I follow are in sequence and my short-term rules are:

$ *Rule 1:* Find sectors that are outperforming the rest of the market.

$ *Rule 2:* Choose the top stocks within that sector.

$ *Rule 3:* Determine which stocks are in an uptrend.

$ *Rule 4:* Buy the stock that seems to be consistently increasing in price.

$ *Rule 5:* Set my sell rules immediately.

So, the first thing I do is narrow down the field. You might like to trade the whole market or just a section of the market, but I concentrate on companies listed in the S&P/ASX 300 only; sometimes even just the S&P/ASX 200 is enough. Choosing from more than 300 charts is a little overwhelming (and I'd rather spend my time reading magazines—not spending days poring over charts).

The gist of the jargon

S&P: Standard & Poor's is a service provider that calculates many of the indices listed on the Australian Securities Exchange and around the world. For example, the S&P/ASX 100 is a list of the top 100 companies listed on the ASX by market capitalisation.

Lazy girl's guide to short-term investing

You've probably already realised by reading this chapter so far that there's a lot more work involved in choosing which shares to buy when it comes to short-term investing. It's much more hands-on than for long-term investing, which is essentially just about checking a few financial figures and then buying.

With short-term investing you need to keep track of which sectors are performing well, which stocks within those sectors are rising and, of course, even when you buy you need to keep a close eye on them to make sure they continue to rise. Phew. It's enough to make any lazy girl run for the sofa and turn on *MasterChef* instead.

But never fear because technology is your friend. Yes, you can set up alerts on your phone, iPad or email to be notified about certain conditions. You can even get apps so that you can see charts and price movements right there on screen.

In addition, most online brokers allow you to set up conditional trading rules, which will enable trades to take place without you having to even be at your computer. So, for example, if you want to sell once your share reaches a profit of 15 per cent you can set up a conditional trading rule and when the trigger happens it will place your order for you automatically.

There are usually four types of triggers that you can set up: falling sell, rising sell, falling buy and rising buy. I personally don't use all of them; I usually just use falling sell and rising sell as these fit into my rules so well.

Falling sell is really just a fancy name for your stop loss. You'll learn later in this chapter how to set your stop-loss price, so once you've determineed this you can go and set up a falling sell trigger that will automatically sell your shares if they fall by a certain amount (say 10 per cent). This way you can get out early if the share goes against you and you'll only lose a small amount of your investment. Using stop-loss strategies is what saved most people from losing all their money during the last market crash.

The rising sell fits well into my rules because it equates very well to my profit sell price (which you determine once you've purchased the shares). It basically states that if the price increases to a certain amount (perhaps 15 per cent above what you paid for it, or whatever profit you determine is realistic for that company), then it will trigger that your order will be placed into the market.

This is different from just placing an order in the market to sell at a certain price because often the ASX will purge any orders that are too far away from the current trading price. However, if you set up conditional trading rules, the trigger will only place the order once the specific rules are met.

The other two common triggers are rising buy and falling buy. These can be useful as well, especially if you're interested in buying into a company but the price is too high and you're waiting for it to come down a bit first. You can set a falling buy so that when the price hits a certain point below what it currently is, you can buy into it. Or, you can set a rising buy, where you can buy into a stock as it's rising. You could use this trigger if, for example, you're not sure whether the stock is in a sideways pattern and if, as soon as it breaks through the 'price barrier', you want to buy in (because that means it's possibly about to go into an uptrend).

Personally, while I do generally use triggers for selling shares automatically, I generally prefer to get SMS alerts for shares that I'm thinking about buying, rather than setting up triggers for buying on my behalf.

However, having conditional trading rules definitely frees up a lot of your time and takes you away from the computer—time that for us time-poor women can be used to do other more exciting things, like secretly opening that Tim Tam packet and hiding it in the back of the fridge so the kids don't find it. Hey, I never said investing was glamorous.

Rule 1: look at the outperforming sectors

The companies listed on the stock exchange are broken down into categories (or sectors). The first thing I always look at when choosing shares for short-term investing is which sectors are outperforming the market. This information can usually be found online, through your broker, from the ASX website or in the sharemarket section of your newspaper.

The main sectors broken down by market capitalisation are:

💲 S&P/ASX 20

💲 S&P/ASX 50

💲 S&P/ASX 100

💲 S&P/ASX 200

💲 S&P/ASX 300

💲 S&P/ASX Midcap 50

💲 S&P/ASX Small Ordinaries.

The main sectors broken down by type of company are:

💲 S&P/ASX Consumer Discretionary

💲 S&P/ASX Consumer Staples

💲 S&P/ASX Energy

💲 S&P/ASX Financials

💲 S&P/ASX Financials excluding Property Trusts

💲 S&P/ASX Health Care

💲 S&P/ASX Industrials

💲 S&P/ASX Information Technology

💲 S&P/ASX Materials

💲 S&P/ASX Property Trusts

💲 S&P/ASX Telecommunication Services

💲 S&P/ASX Utilities.

I look for sectors that have been doing well for at least three months. This is so that I can be more confident that they will continue to perform well in the following months. I usually end up with a list that looks something like table 5.1.

Table 5.1: S&P/ASX indices—percentage change between 29 November 2010 and 25 February 2011

Sector	29 Nov 2010	25 Feb 2011	Percentage change
Energy (XEJ)	15 391	16 245	5.5%
Materials (XMJ)	13 387	14 113	5.4%
Industrials (XNJ)	3 704	3 774	1.9%
Cons Discretionary (XDJ)	1 498	1 517	1.3%
Cons Staples (XSJ)	7 742	7 873	1.7%
Health Care (XHJ)	8 733	8 714	−0.2%
Financials (XFJ)	4 263	4 561	7.0%
Info Tech (XIJ)	603	593	−1.7%
Telecomms (XTJ)	979	961	−1.8%
Utilities (XUJ)	4 423	4 228	−4.4%
A-REIT (XPJ)	847	875	3.2%
Fin excl. Prop (XXJ)	4 920	5 299	7.7%
Index	29 Nov 2010	25 Feb 2011	Percentage change
S&P/ASX 20 (XTL)	2 762	2 902	5.1%
S&P/ASX 50 (XFL)	4 592	4 809	4.7%
S&P/ASX 100 (XTO)	3 759	3 936	4.7%
S&P/ASX 200 (XJO)	4 619	4 837	4.7%

Table 5.1 shows that over the three months up to 25 February 2011 the best performing sector within the S&P/ASX 200 was

Financials excl. Property with a 7.7 per cent increase, followed by Financials with an increase of 7.0 per cent.

Any sector that was doing better than the All Ords would be considered worthy of further investigation, but most of the time I stick with the top two or three sectors I've worked out myself or found listed in the financial section of the newspaper, simply because I find that looking at no more than these few sectors is manageable for me, and there are enough stocks in these sectors to help me decide what I want to buy.

Rule 2: top stocks in that sector

By the time you get to rule 2, you've already eliminated a whole swag of companies (which is great for us lazy girls because we then don't need to look at many companies). The next thing I do is look at stocks within a sector to see which are outperforming which. It's a funny thing about the sharemarket—some stocks in the same sector seem to ride on the coat tails of others that are doing well. It seems that if, say, some energy stocks are doing well, the rest seem to do okay too. This is just a general observation and it doesn't happen in all cases, but you'd be surprised how often it does seem to be the case.

Once I've narrowed down the top stocks in the sectors I'm interested in, I have a list of a dozen or so candidates that might look like table 5.2.

From this list I can see which stocks in the sector Fin excl. Prop (XXJ)—which we determined in rule 1 was the best performing sector—have been consistently increasing in price over the past three months and which ones have not. As you would expect, there are some very attractive looking returns here after just three months.

The shares I generally choose to look at further are those that have shown returns above the average price of the sector as a whole.

Table 5.2: list of candidates

Company	30 Nov 10	28 Feb 11	Percentage change
AMP	5.05	5.31	5.1%
ANZ	22.66	24.13	6.5%
ASX	37.82	36.42	–3.7%
AXA	6.17	6.34	2.8%
BEN	9.88	9.36	–5.3%
BOQ	11.60	9.85	–15.1%
CBA	48.28	53.11	10.0%
CGF	4.42	5.06	14.5%
FKP	0.84	0.87	3.6%
HGG	1.97	2.59	31.5%
IAG	3.77	3.65	–3.2%
IFL	7.18	7.78	8.4%
LLC	7.58	9.12	20.3%
MQG	35.45	37.87	6.8%
NAB	23.45	25.80	10.0%
PPT	35.52	32.34	–9.0%
PTM	5.08	4.64	–8.7%
QBE	16.83	18.14	7.8%
SUN	9.03	8.42	–6.8%
TAL	2.65	3.93	48.3%
WBC	21.37	23.53	10.1%

So, in this example, XXJ had an average return of 7.7 per cent over the past three months. From our findings, the companies that contributed to this were:

$ CBA at 10 per cent

$ CGF at 14.5 per cent

$ HGG at 31.5 per cent

$ IFL at 8.4 per cent

$ LLC at 20.3 per cent

$ NAB at 10 per cent

$ QBE at 7.8 per cent

$ TAL at 48.3 per cent

$ WBC at 10.1 per cent.

Be careful not to automatically choose the company that has the highest return, though, because it could be that it's at the end of its uptrend. We really need to investigate further to see which of our list we want to put our money into.

Because we're only interested in the short term here (a few months at the most), you'll probably notice a lot of increases and decreases in price over a short period of time. Some stocks are very volatile—up one month, down the next—but I prefer to choose stocks that are more consistent so that, if they go up one month I'm fairly confident that they'll go up the next month as well. Some share investors love volatile stocks and go out of their way to try to take advantage of share-price movements (buying when they go down and selling when they go back up). Choose whichever method suits you, but I'll continue talking about the more consistent companies.

Rule 3: look for an uptrend

Once I have a handful of stocks to choose from, I check their prices and charts to see which seem to consistently do well. I see whether they're in a clear uptrend so that I can be confident that they'll probably remain so, at least over the next few days or weeks that I'm going to hold them for. I check whether there seems to be increasing volume on bullish days and decreased volume on bearish days, and I check the latest company announcements to see whether there was a reason for the uptrend.

Spotting an uptrend is usually fairly easy: you just look at the chart. However, sometimes it can be better to draw a trendline on a chart to confirm your observation (see figure 5.4 on p. 93). Use whichever method suits your style best. Figures 5.8 (overleaf) and 5.9 (on p. 111) show charts from the list of stocks I'm interested in.

As you can see, while the three-month return on CBA looked healthy at 10 per cent, it may be that it's at the end of its uptrend since it has broken down through its 20-day EMA. That's why it's important to confirm prices by looking at the charts before you buy.

LLC (see figure 5.9), on the other hand, looks like it's still continuing its uptrend. Its prices are above (or hugging) the 20-day EMA and volume seems to be expanding on bullish days. While there are still a few more checks to do before you buy, it could be that Lend Lease will make a great short-term investment.

Rule 4: choose the most consistent companies

As with long-term investing, I like consistency in the stocks I choose. I don't like volatile stocks that jump around too much. Some people like these stocks and use strategies for buying when the price jumps low and selling when the price jumps high, but I'm a much more cautious person when it comes to choosing my short-term investments. I usually follow a very simple rule: buy what's going up and sell what's going down.

From looking at the charts of stocks, I can usually see at a glance which appear to be the most consistent. Those that seem to be in a clear uptrend are usually the ones I choose to buy.

Figure 5.8: CBA shows that it might have finished its uptrend as it crosses down through the 20-day EMA

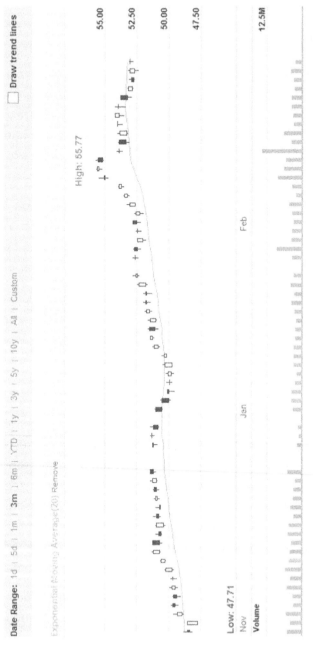

COMMONWEALTH BANK. FPO

Date Range: 1d | 5d | 1m | 3m | 6m | YTD | 1y | 3y | 5y | 10y | All | Custom   ☐ **Draw trend lines**

Exponential Moving Average(20) Remove

High: 55.77

55.00

52.50

50.00

47.50

Low: 47.71

Nov   Jan   Feb

Volume   12.5M

Source: <www.CommSec.com.au>

Figure 5.9: LLC chart with 20-day EMA in an uptrend
LEND LEASE GROUP STAPLED

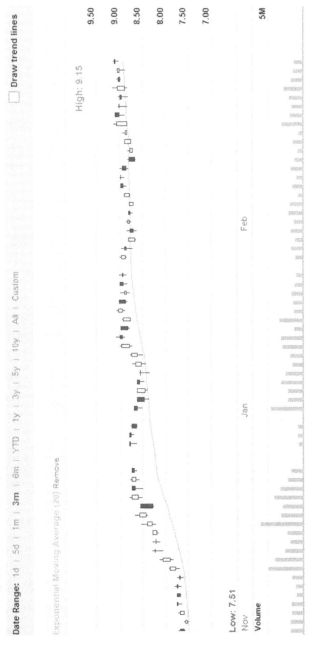

Source: <www.CommSec.com.au>

111

I may look at why the share price is increasing: has the company expanded its distribution or has profit increased substantially over the past six months? Half the time I have no idea why a share price might be increasing, although it seems awfully suspicious when the volume and the price seem to increase for no apparent reason until a few weeks later when a favourable announcement about the company emerges (did a lot of people know something that I didn't—hmmm?). But mostly I don't really care about the 'why' when I buy for the short term; I really only care whether the share I buy will go up in price or not.

From my list of stocks in table 5.2, the most consistent (with not much difference between last month's per cent increase and this month's per cent increase) are shown in table 5.3.

Table 5.3: most consistent performers

Company	30 Dec 2010	31 Jan 2011	28 Feb 2011	Dec–Jan	Jan–Feb
CBA	51.27	52.46	53.11	2.3%	1.2%
NAB	23.70	24.66	25.80	4.1%	4.6%
TAL	3.87	3.91	3.93	1.0%	0.5%
WBC	22.21	22.99	23.53	3.5%	2.3%

NAB and WBC seem the more stable and consistent, and they deliver good monthly returns that I'd be thrilled to receive.

Rule 5: set your sell price

I've known a few people who are obsessed with buying at the right price. I personally don't think the buy price is nearly as important as the sell price when I'm investing for short term. I don't see the point in worrying over a few cents' difference when you find a good stock to buy. The sell price is where you either make your profit or get out early so you don't lose too much of your hard-earnt cash.

I think the sell price is the most important element when buying for the short term. You can avoid losing your hard-earnt investment money by getting out early when the share price looks as if it's going against you, or take your profit when the share price does go according to plan. You take your profit and run (unless, of course, the share doesn't seem to be slowing so you hold on for the ride—but more about that later).

The first thing you need to do after you make your purchase is to set your sell rules immediately. Usually I set two sell rules: the stop-loss sell price and the profit sell price.

Stop-loss sell price

My first sell price is the stop loss. This is the price at which you sell out immediately if your share seems to fall as soon as you buy it (and some of them do unfortunately!). I usually set my stop loss approximately 10 per cent below the price I paid for the share. This is my 'insurance', so to speak. If a share price turns against me, I'll only ever lose that 10 per cent. That way most of my capital remains intact and it means I'm still in the game. I think most people's fear with regard to the stock market is that they'll lose all of their money, but fortunately the sharemarket isn't like betting on a horse. With gambling, you either win or lose and you either get your money back or you drown your sorrows at the bar. With shares it's rare for a company to disappear overnight; most of the time the stock price decreases over a period of days and weeks before bottoming out, so you have a chance to get some or most of your money back before the going gets catastrophic.

The gist of the jargon

Stop loss: A predetermined price point at which you're prepared to sell your shares to reduce your loss.

Don't fall into the trap of thinking that if you just hold on a bit longer the share price might go back up. If the price falls to your stop-loss sell price, there's only one thing to do and that's *sell*. There were plenty of times when I sold a stock that had dropped too low for my comfort level, only for the share price to turn around the next week and spurt forward again. If I hadn't sold I wouldn't have made a loss on that stock. On the other hand, there were even more times when I was happy I sold because over the coming weeks the price fell even further. Can you really be sure that the price is going to turn around? Unless you have a crystal ball, I don't think anyone can be certain what will happen so it's better to be safe than sorry and sell up when the stock falls to your set price.

You can always get back into a stock if it turns good again, but it's not so easy to make your money back if your stock falls further and you didn't get out early enough.

As I mentioned earlier in this chapter, you can actually pre-set your stop-loss price automatically with most online brokers. You can usually find the conditional trading order under the 'Orders' tab; then you choose 'Conditional orders'. I find setting my stop-loss order by setting up a trigger saves me a lot of time.

Profit sell price

The second sell price is the price I expect a stock to rise to over a predetermined period of time. Each stock is different and I determine this price based on the stock's past behaviour.

Let's say that a stock I was interested in had increased in price an average of 6 per cent per month over the past three months, with three months being the maximum length of time I was happy to hold this particular stock. I would then probably set my sell price at 18 or 19 per cent above what I paid for it. Of course, there are exceptions, but generally I would set my profit sell based on past performance.

Example

Starting share price: $1.00

Month	1	=	$1.00	+	6%	=	$1.06
Month	2	=	$1.06	+	6%	=	$1.12
Month	3	=	$1.12	+	6%	=	$1.19

Total gain over three months = 19%

It's possible that the share price might meet your sell target a lot sooner than three months, and it's also possible it will never reach your sell target within the time frame. I would sell the stock if it reached the profit level early or once the time limit was up. Sometimes, despite the time limit being up, I may give a stock a bit longer to reach the expected profit level in case the company had a bad month or its shares were in the middle of going ex dividend or for some other reason. But I usually let a stock go no more than an extra month.

I'll use the examples from the list in table 5.3 and assume we went ahead and purchased both National Australia Bank (NAB) and Westpac Bank (WBC), since our research showed us they were the best bets at the time. Our sell prices would be as follows.

Example

National Australia Bank

Bought 127 shares at $23.70 = $3009.90

Sell price: stop loss $23.70 − 10% = $21.33

Profit sell $23.70 + 10% (what I think it could achieve over three months) = $26.07

Westpac Bank

Bought 136 shares at $22.21 = $3020.56

Sell price: stop loss $22.21 − 10% = $19.98

Profit sell $22.21 + 10.1% = $24.45

The first thing I do is set the stop-loss price at 10 per cent below the price I paid (as shown above). The second thing to do is set the profit sell price. This is different for each stock and is how much, on average, I think the share price might go up, based on past performance. NAB's price rose by 10 per cent over the past three months (as we worked out from table 5.2), so I could reasonably assume that, if it remains consistent, it might rise by about the same percentage again over the next two to three months. Likewise, WBC's price rose 10.1 per cent over the previous three months so it might reach another 10 per cent over the next three months if it remains consistent.

If you bought $3000 worth of shares in each company, you could make a nice profit of $300 from National Australia Bank and $305 from Westpac, for a total profit of $605 over the time period—quite a good return on investment for only three months (many people are lucky to make this over a year). Of course, you might be wrong as well, and the share prices might fall to your stop-loss sell, which is why it's important to have both sell prices in place.

While past performance is no guarantee of future performance, it will give you a good guide as to where to set your profit sell.

And again, you can actually pre-set your profit sell price automatically with conditional trading rules. It can be really good knowing that you've just made a nice profit and the money is going to be in your bank account in a few days (trade day plus three). I usually receive an SMS alert when the conditional order has gone through successfully so I know as soon as it happens.

Dividend strategies

You're probably wondering why I'm including a section on dividends in the short-term section as usually dividends are associated with long-term investing. Well, there are some tricks you can use if you're a short-term investor to take advantage of the patterns that share prices seem to follow at ex-dividend time.

Many times, when buying shares on short-term rules, you aren't concerned with receiving dividends. However, if you find a stock that's about to pay out dividends and is also in a clear uptrend you might want to try taking advantage of the price movements during this time.

Normally, once a company announces it's going to pay a dividend on a certain date, there's increased buying in that share. Very often, the share price will increase (especially if the dividend is fully franked) up until the ex-dividend date, when it falls by approximately one and a half times the value of the dividend.

Then, over the next two or three weeks, it increases again until it's at the level it was before the fall. If your stock does show this characteristic behaviour you could take advantage of it by:

$ buying the shares once the company announces the ex-dividend date and holding them until a few days before the ex-dividend date—and then selling (hopefully making a nice profit)

117

§ realising that you won't actually get the dividend as you weren't holding at the right time, but accepting that that isn't your plan here

§ buying into the stock again after the share price falls (usually the day the share goes ex dividend, but sometimes the following few days) and waiting for it to increase in price to the level it was at before the ex-dividend date, again making a small profit.

So how do you find out when a stock is going ex dividend? Usually a company pays dividends at around the same time each year, so if it paid in March and October last year, it will probably do the same again this year. Most online stockbrokers also list upcoming dividend payments in the news and research sections of their website.

Example

Have a look at figure 5.10, which shows Bradken Limited's behaviour around ex-dividend day.

While every company exhibits different patterns around the time the share goes ex dividend, what most often happens is that there's increased buying in the weeks leading up to the date, followed by a fall in price and then an increase again a few weeks later. In the example shown for Bradken Limited, we can see that the share did fall in price after it went ex dividend in mid August.

It fell even further in the week following the ex-dividend date (which was probably due to all the shareholders getting rid of the stock since they were now eligible for the dividend and didn't need to hold it any longer). However, it then rose again (and even higher than before) in the following weeks.

Figure 5.10: BKN chart showing a fall in price when the share goes ex dividend on 16 August 2010

BRADKEN LIMITED FPO

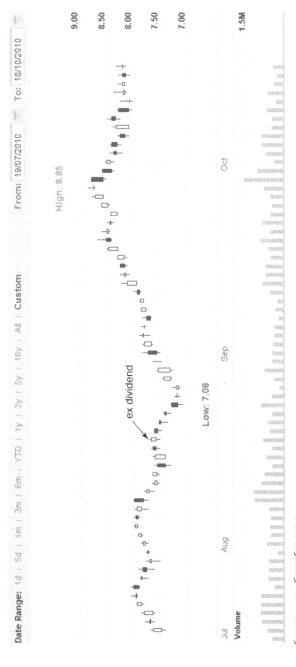

Source: <www.CommSec.com.au>

Example

If you'd taken advantage of these price increases using the dividend strategy I've outlined, your return might have looked something like this.

Buy prior to the share going ex dividend:
5 July 2010 — BUY 1000 shares of BKN at $7.41 = $7410
Sell a few days prior to the ex-dividend date:
SELL 1000 shares of BKN at $7.63 = $7630 (profit $220)
Buy after the share went ex dividend:
23 August 2010 — BUY 1000 shares of BKN at $7.20 = $7200
Sell four weeks later:
SELL 1000 shares of BKN at $8.42 = $8420 (profit of $1220)

This makes an overall profit of $1440 (just under 20 per cent over two to three months) — not bad for a few weeks' work, eh? Of course, not every stock will exhibit these same characteristics around its ex-dividend day. If you're going to try this strategy, make sure the stock is already in an uptrend (or in a sideways band such as the one displayed by Bradken Limited), and check out the stock's behaviour last time it went ex dividend to see whether it displayed similar patterns.

Takeovers

Another interesting strategy for short-term players is investing in takeover bids. A takeover is basically when one company makes an attempt to buy another company. Sometimes the takeover is agreed upon between the two parties and is a friendly takeover bid; other times the other company doesn't want to be taken over and a battle will ensue (often called a hostile takeover bid).

For one company to take over another, it must buy more than 20 per cent of the company. The buying company can do this either by buying shares in the company it wants to purchase through the stock exchange (an on-market bid), or by sending letters to current shareholders offering to buy their shares from them (an off-market bid).

Often, more than one company might want to buy the target company and this is where it gets more interesting. If two or more companies are battling it out to buy the target company, they'll often start offering more money to shareholders, and obviously the longer you hold the shares, the more the price increases—possibly through the roof! Even when there's only one bidder wanting to buy into a target company, if the original offer is rejected by the company the bidder will often increase its offer.

As soon as a takeover bid is announced (either by announcements to the ASX or through reports in the financial section of newspapers), you should buy into the company that's being fought over, especially if the price on the market is less than the offered price (then you're guaranteed to get at least the offered price if the takeover is successful). Often, the price on the market is about the same as the offer price, in which case I would still buy into the stock in case the offer price is increased or another company offers more money and a bidding war starts.

The first offer in a takeover bid is rarely the last and, if you want to try investing into takeover bid strategies, you should consider holding on until the end to see how high the price will go!

Strategy for takeover bids

As soon as a takeover bid is announced it will be all over the newspapers, so it's doubtful you'll miss it if you're keeping an eye on the financial section. Once it's been announced, many buyers will scramble to buy into the company under offer so don't be surprised if the price increases dramatically straightaway. Don't worry—as long as you buy close to the first price offered in the bid you should be fine. Even if no other offers are forthcoming, you'll break even.

However, the first bid is very rarely the last, especially if a few parties get involved in wanting to own the company in play. All you need to do is sit back and enjoy the ride. During this time you may receive lots of letters in the mail offering to buy your shares at certain prices; I don't recommend you fill in any of them agreeing to sell until the very end when the last bid is made.

Usually that's about a week or a few days before the closing date for the final bid offer. Even if the final date comes and goes and the bid is successful, your shares will be sold for you and you'll receive your proceeds in the mail. (So in this case being lazy is actually worth your while.)

Sometimes during a takeover bid you won't just receive a cash offer for your shares; you might be offered shares in the bidder's company (the company offering to buy or take over the other company) instead (called scrip), or possibly even a combination of cash and scrip.

If and when you finally decide to sell or accept the takeover offer you can either sell on the market as with any normal shareholding, sign the letter that the bidder sent you and return it to them (so that you won't have to pay brokerage costs), or simply wait until the shares are eventually sold for you (although often you won't get your money for at least four weeks after the closing date if you do it this way).

> **The gist of the jargon**
>
> **Scrip:** When one company offers you shares in its own company in return for shares in another company.

$ $ $

Short-term investing can be a lot of fun for those (like me) who like to watch the market and take advantage of weekly price fluctuations, but it isn't for everyone. There's no doubt that investing for the short term can be risky, even if you do have your stop-loss plan in place.

The three main ways to invest using short-term methods are:

$ analysing stocks that are increasing in price

$ using dividend strategies

$ buying into takeover bids.

Short-term trading can be a good way to learn quickly about the market ups and downs. And all education is good if it eventually increases your bottom line. That's what we're investing for, after all!

Taking the first step

Chapter 6

By now you should be ready to get started. You've saved up enough money. Your brokerage account is open and ready to go. You've decided which investment style you're going to use. You've got a plan in place and a handful of companies you're ready to invest in.

So what's stopping you? If you're anything like me, then taking that first step can be a nerve-wracking prospect. It took me a few months and many books before I actually made my first investment, but now that I have I'm truly glad I made that decision as it has improved my financial position and knowledge significantly.

That's what I want for you too: to help you take control of your financial destiny and become a savvy investor. Take a deep breath because it's time for you to take that leap.

Should I paper trade first?

Often, the hardest thing about investing can be taking that first jump into the market. Many people trade on paper without ever once committing their own money or making that first investment. Paper trading or writing down what you 'probably would' spend and the trades you 'probably might' take is a popular pastime for some would-be investors. I've had many friends who've said to me, 'I knew Rio Tinto was going to do well and if I had put all my funds into it I'd have tripled my money by now'. I usually respond with, 'If you were so confident then why didn't you?'

I'm not a huge fan of paper trading—I think people tend to act differently once their own money is involved. In my experience it seems that people are prepared to take more risks and take less time researching when they're using hypothetical money. If you feel more comfortable 'practising', then by all means go ahead, but paper trading can never come close to the thrill of actually placing your first order with your own money and watching your investment move in the market.

If you decide to 'pretend' trade, you should do it for three or four months. Any longer than that and you'll probably get bored and give up. One or two months is an ideal time frame as it will give you confidence in your strategies. Get yourself an exercise book and line up a page with the following columns and headings:

Starting capital: $_____
How many different companies: _____
How much to invest per stock: $_____

Make sure you decide beforehand how much you want to spend on each stock and how many different stocks you want to hold so that you can keep it as realistic as possible. It also helps to write notes on why you chose that particular company so that you can remember your thinking behind each share purchase and learn what works for you. Table 6.1 (overleaf) shows the information you might like to record.

Table 6.1: information for a paper trade

Date	Stock	No. of shares	Buy price $	Value $	Current price $	Current value $	Profit/ loss $	%
Example								
13/09/2010	EQN	1000	5.49	5490	5.80	5800	310	6

Investing on paper only really works for short-term strategies. I don't know anyone who has paper traded using long-term investment strategies—after all it would take you a few years before you knew whether your investments were paying off or not. You could always look back over a period of time to see whether your strategies 'would have' worked, but who knows whether you'd really have chosen that particular stock back then anyway? In my mind, looking backwards is called research, not hindsight.

The only time I paper trade is if I'm testing new strategies that I'm not confident about yet. I'll often paper trade a dozen different strategies at once to discover which one works best for me, then constantly tweak it until it suits my style and seems to provide consistent profits. That's how I came up with the short-term strategies I've outlined in this book: I played around with a few different methods until I found those that worked best for me.

Another really fun way to try your strategies out is to find out when the ASX holds its sharemarket games. They usually hold a few games each year and you get an imaginary trading account of $50 000 to invest over a period of two or three months. You can only trade with a certain list of shares (usually those in the S&P/ ASX 100), so it's limited in that respect, and there are rules such as how much of your money you can hold in one particular company and so forth, but it should give you a sense of what it's really like to put money into the stock market. There are also prizes for those from each state who come first, second and third. It's certainly fun to play, but for some reason I seem to do worse in those games than I do in my real investing (and thank goodness for that!).

How it feels — the joy of making your first investment

I've noticed that many people — and I was no exception — usually go through a range of emotions with their very first investment. First, you're proud of yourself for finally making that first step — woohoo, I'm a stockholder! Then, the moment you place your order a sense of panic sets in. Did I do the right thing? What happens if I lose all my money? This is usually about the time that you become obsessed with watching the market closely for constant validation that you made the right choice. How stressful is that! Luckily things get better after that first share. The first stock I purchased was Oroton. I was so proud of my little shares that I'd watch the price move every five minutes. My mood jumped from elation when the price went up, to near depression when it dropped. I originally bought it using long-term investing rules, but was watching it so much that it was beginning to become an obsession. I would even go into Oroton stores in my lunch break to make sure people were buying their purses and handbags; after all, I owned a piece of the company, and I had to make sure everything was running smoothly!

After that first share, I don't think I could even name the next 20 or so that I bought. I started to become very businesslike about it — if a stock fitted my criteria, it was a buy. If it didn't fit anymore, I'd sell. Once I took my emotions out of the equation,

I started to become a very savvy investor. My strategies were working!

No doubt, taking that first step is scary. Often you're so terrified of losing everything that you delay placing your first order. You see your stock's price go up and feel annoyed with yourself for not going ahead sooner. But it doesn't really matter if you miss one opportunity; there's plenty of time and there are plenty of companies. If you miss one, there will be many more to come. If you use the strategies outlined in this book and your worst fears are realised (you buy and the price does go against you), you'll probably lose only a small portion of your money. While it's a loss, it's not the end of the world; you can make it up again later when you choose a successful company.

What to expect when you place your first trade

Most people expect that their very first investment is going to make them rich. I had grand visions of the multimillion dollar house I was going to live in by the sea, and the people I would hire to cook my food and do my laundry, and that it would all happen in three short years if I consistently made 10 per cent per month. Ah yes, what a life of luxury I would live, sunbaking by my perfectly landscaped pool ... *crash—back to reality!* While I'm much more financially secure than I was five years ago, no-one cooks for me except my partner, when he's feeling generous. And while I do consider myself a successful investor, I know that not every trade is going to turn golden.

There's no way that every stock you choose will be successful. I certainly don't always choose the right companies. Many of the shares I hold seem to do nothing and sit at the same price for what seems like an eternity. Some shares even decrease in price, but that doesn't worry me as I have a sound plan in place and my profits more than make up for my losses. When I started out, for every four stocks that I bought, one decreased in price, two remained steady and one increased. This varied according to whether it was a bull or bear market. Now I'm doing a bit better, but we all have to start somewhere, so if you start with similar results to mine, this is what a typical month (or year, depending on your time frame) may look like for you.

Example

Let's say you have a starting capital of $8000, and you choose to invest $2000 in four different companies:

Stock 1: $2000. Decreases by 10 per cent and you sell. Final amount: $1800
Stock 2: $2000. Remains the same price. Final amount: $2000
Stock 3: $2000. Increases by 5 per cent. Final amount: $2100
Stock 4: $2000. Increases by 15 per cent. Final amount: $2300
Ending capital: $8200
Profit: $200

You had one stock that decreased in price to your stop-loss sell, so you sold at a loss of $200. The following two stocks either didn't move at all or moved only a small amount, giving you a profit of $100, and the last stock met your expectations and you made a profit of $300. That brings your total profit to $200. While a profit of $200 is an increase of only 2 per cent and is not going to make you rich (unless you could do this every month), it's certainly a start and hopefully once you become more experienced and confident you'll be able to build up to even bigger profits.

Case study: Kylie's first three months

Kylie was excited about starting to invest and she had a cool $9000 to begin with. She had learned my tips for short-term investing and made the decision that she was going to purchase three different stocks, buying $3000 worth of shares in each one. This is what her buy orders looked like at the time.

RDF	810	3.70	$2997
MAP	997	3.01	$3001
AAC	1987	1.51	$3000
Total value			**$8998**

At the end of the first month this is what her portfolio looked like:

RDF	810	3.89	$3150
MAP	997	3.19	$3180
AAC	1987	1.66	$3298
Total value			**$9628**

At the end of the second month:

RDF	810	4.00	$3240
MAP	997	3.45	$3439
AAC	1987	1.86	$3695
Total value			**$10374**

At the end of the third and final month:

RDF	810	4.05	$3280
MAP	997	3.12	$3110
AAC	1987	1.73	$3437
Total value			**$9827**

Kylie had decided to sell after three months, and at the end of the three-month period she had made a very decent profit of $1827 (less brokerage), which she was ecstatic about. If she'd left it in her high interest bearing account (and she very nearly did), which was paying 5.25 per cent per annum at the time, she would have only made about one hundred dollars for the three-month period. That's a massive difference. Of course, she would have made even more if she had sold in February; however, she wasn't to know that at the time. And besides, who really cares: she 'd made just over $1800 in only three months — that's certainly nothing to be disappointed about! While not every investment she made after this turned out as successfully as her first three stocks (some did just as well; some didn't do very well at all), Kylie didn't continue to hold her losing stocks; she cut her losses early and kept to a good investment plan.

When I was starting out I didn't have access to all the hints and tips that I've included in this book, so hopefully you'll be much better off than I was in the beginning!

Once you place your first order, it will take about four business days for the money to come out of your account for that trade. It depends on whether you're placing your orders within market hours or not, but generally the transaction will take place on trade day plus three business days. The first time I placed a trade I didn't realise this, and was perplexed as to why the money was still in my account two days later even though I technically owned the shares — did I get them for free? By the end of the week the money had been taken out of my account. Remember that this is happening and don't spend it beforehand!

The same applies when selling your shares; you won't actually get the money until trade day plus three business days. This can be interesting as you could essentially buy and sell within that three- or four-day period without any money trading hands. That's what some very short term traders actually do, even buying and selling in the same day, but I've never been successful in such a short period. They never have to put up the money because they never hold the stock until the settlement date. I wouldn't recommend that you actually do this unless you have the money as a backup because it's too risky a strategy. Imagine if your stock went down in price instead.

What's a realistic profit?

Ahh, the million dollar question. Well, to be honest I have no idea what will be a realistic profit for you. It depends on how much capital you have to start with and what sort of risk you're prepared to take. Remember that on average the stock market professionals are happy if they make above 10 per cent per annum. I think if you're doing better than that, you should be very happy with yourself.

I actually think it's easier for the average investor to outperform the professionals because we're usually trading with a smaller amount of capital. Think about it: if you've got $500 000 to invest in a company, you're going to have a harder time investing than if you have only $5000. You can move a lot more quickly with smaller amounts of money as you don't have to wait for multiple buy and sell orders for your transaction to take place. Also, trying to invest $500 000 will probably move the market against you. As your buy order goes through, the price will probably rise and you'll end up buying at a higher price. Likewise, trying to offload $500 000 worth of shares will probably move the share price lower and you'll make a decreased profit.

Usually, with that amount of money, the professionals (such as those trading for a managed fund with huge amounts of money to deal with) will buy over a period of a few days or a few weeks so that they don't move the market too much. They don't have the luxury of getting in and out quickly as we do and, therefore, can't take advantage of quick profits.

The way I measure whether I'm making a realistic profit is by looking at whether my account size is increasing or not. It's really that simple. It doesn't even have to increase by a large amount (although I usually do a happy dance if it is). If I finish with more money than I started with, then I judge that month or that trade successful. If it reaches the profit level that I set beforehand, then I know I'm doing well.

I don't measure my investing by the dollar amount I'm making or by whether or not I beat last month's increase (who needs that pressure — investing is stressful enough). As long as I'm making profits and successful trades I feel I must be doing something right.

$ $ $

Investing is an exciting game, but unless you're prepared to jump in and actually make your first investment you'll never know what it's really like to be an investor. Paper trading is certainly fun, but I think you'll be a better investor when you actually use your own money. The decisions you make and the level of risk you take when your own money is involved is often quite different from what happens on paper. Keeping your expectations realistic and making consistent profits is the key to stock market success. If you can do this, you'll be surprised where you find yourself in a few short years.

Yay! My shares went up!

Chapter 7

You've just invested $3000 in your first stock and your fingers and toes are crossed hoping for the best. You decide to check in about a week later, just to see how it's doing. Oh my God, it's increased in price. I'm rich! I'm rich! First off, congratulations! You've made a profit! Well, on paper anyway. Now you need to decide what to do next. Do you sell or hold? My answer is ... it depends.

Choosing when to take a profit

When a share first increases in price, often a mixture of emotions surface and you feel a combination of elation and terror at the same time. Sometimes it's just as scary when the price rises as it is when it falls!

Questions start to swirl through your brain. Should I take the profit now? What happens if it goes back down again? What happens if I take the profit and it rises further and I miss out on a bigger opportunity? While you'll never know the perfect time to sell your shares (except with hindsight), having a plan will make the decision process a lot easier. Knowing when to take the profit and when to let the share run comes down to a number of factors:

$ *Did you buy on long- or short-term rules?* Very often the answer to this single question is enough for you to decide whether you should continue to hold.

$ *Are you happy with the profit?* It might not be thousands of dollars, but is the share even capable of reaching such heights?

$ *Do you need the money?* Or more importantly do you need the money right now?

$ *What does the share chart look like?* Does it look like it has reached the end of its profit run or do you think it still has some steam in it?

$ *Do you know the reason for the share's increase in price?* Very often you don't know, but if the company just stumbled upon some amazing new technology, for example, it might be worth hanging on to see its potential.

It's extremely important to be businesslike about holding shares and not get too emotional, otherwise you can fall into the trap of waiting too long or selling too early. (I know it's nearly impossible not to get too emotional, especially when you're starting out in the market but, trust me, it gets easier the longer you invest.)

On the next few pages I'll try to help you decide whether you should continue to hold your shares or whether it's best to take your profit now and break out the champagne.

If you bought using long-term investment rules

If your shares were bought using long-term investment rules, I'd generally say, 'No, don't sell yet'. You'll no doubt experience many highs and lows in the share price during its long-term journey. Sometimes during market highs it's easy to get caught up in the excitement of making a paper profit and wanting to spend that profit on a new Prada purse (we've all been there), but if all is well you should think about continuing to hold the shares and sitting back to enjoy the ride (and the dividends) for a long time yet.

Long-term investors have the advantage of not having to ask the 'Is it the right time to sell?' question that short-term players have to ask themselves because the answer is usually quite simple. If you bought on long-term investing rules, you should hold for the long term (in most cases). Short-term players usually need to ask that question weekly so be pleased that you can avoid that emotional decision making! At least for a while, anyway.

There are only two circumstances where it's acceptable to sell if you bought using long-term investing rules:

$ You need the money for an emergency.

$ The company no longer fits the rules under which you chose the stock in the first place.

Selling because you need the money

Having your money tied up can be a nuisance and a godsend. Impulse buys can be minimised if you don't have the cash right there in your purse to spend, but when you need it and it's tied up in investments it might be time to liquidate some assets.

First, ask yourself whether you *really* need the money. If you need urgent car repairs or would like to put a deposit on a new house and you don't have any other spare cash to use then these are very genuine reasons for selling your shares; however, if you simply want those Tiffany diamond earrings for your office Christmas party, then maybe you need to re-examine your goals for investing to determine whether they're a priority or not.

The gist of the jargon

Liquidate: Convert your paper assets into cash, usually by selling your investments or borrowing money against them.

It can be tempting to take your money out of your investments early, but you'll probably make more money keeping your money in the stock, even if its price increased only 8 per cent for the year. If it does that every year, you'll be very wealthy in a few short years. If you take your money out even for one year, missing out on the compound interest will make a dramatic difference.

Let's say you have $10 000 to invest and that your investments increase in value by 8 per cent every year for five years. In the first example, you leave your money invested and decide to sell only at the end of the five years. In the second example, you decide to withdraw $500 in each of the first two years for 'expenses'.

Example 1 — holding for the entire five years

Purchased: $10 000 worth of shares
Year 1: 8% increase = $10 800
Year 2: 8% increase = $11 664

Year 3: 8% increase = $12597
Year 4: 8% increase = $13604
Year 5: 8% increase = $14693
Total profit = $4693

Example 2 — withdrawing $500 at the end of years 1 and 2

Purchased: $10000 worth of shares
Year 1: 8% increase = $10800 − $500 = $10300
Year 2: 8% increase = $11124 − $500 = $10624
Year 3: 8% increase = $11474
Year 4: 8% increase = $12392
Year 5: 8% increase = $13383
Total profit = $3383

To be fair, you need to take into account the $1000 that you withdrew so, at the end of five years in example 2, you'd have $3383 + $500 + $500 = $4383, which is still $300 less than the profit in example 1. The $300 might not seem much, but the longer you keep your money invested—or if you receive a higher return than just 8 per cent—the more it will add up. Do you really want to miss out on extra money at the end to satisfy a spending desire now?

Selling because the company's financials have changed

Every six or 12 months (when each company's financial statements are released—usually around February and September) you should look over your investments to see whether they still fit the rules under which you bought them. If a company continues to show good profit and its return on equity, earnings and profit still seem stable then I see no reason why you need to sell your holding. One of the easiest ways to decide whether it's still a good company is to ask yourself whether you'd still buy the stock today. If the answer is yes then there's no point selling; hang on and enjoy the ride.

If, however, the financial results have changed substantially, you might need to re-examine your investment. What exactly has changed for this company? Is this setback major or minor? Is it something the company will be able to recover from in a few months? Sometimes a company might report lower than expected earnings but still be a great company financially and worth keeping hold of. Other times it might have increased its debt (or declined on some other financial measure) to a level where you're just not comfortable holding it any more so you decide to sell out.

Let's say you bought shares in a company because it showed a 20 per cent return on equity, it had good stability over the previous five years and its debt-to-equity ratio was 70 per cent. It fit your criteria of a good company at the time and so you purchased a holding. However, the latest annual report shows that the figures don't look so good. The company's return on equity is still okay at 16 per cent but it has increased its borrowings so that its debt-to-equity ratio is above 75 per cent, and because it had a bad year its stability has dropped a bit. The share price is still higher than when you purchased it, but in this instance you might decide that you'll cash in your profit because you're no longer confident about this company's future, and would prefer to invest your money elsewhere.

If you bought using short-term rules

If you bought your shares using short-term rules, it could be time to take that profit, but maybe not. Confused? Well, you'll need to examine your stock a little further before you decide that it's time to sell.

It depends on how much the share price went up. Did it reach your profit sell price? Is this a typical rise for the share? Are you happy taking the profit now even though it might go up still further and you could miss out on further gains? Does the chart indicate that the price is likely to turn back down? As you can see, there are quite a few questions to evaluate before a final sell decision is made. I'll help you explore these further.

In a nutshell, there are two main reasons for selling if you bought using short-term rules. The first rule is if the share *has* hit your profit sell price (although there are still exceptions to this rule as well). The second rule is if the share has increased in price but hasn't quite hit your profit sell point and you're not confident it will get there in the near future as you've held on for twice as long as you planned and it doesn't seem to be gaining any longer.

Selling because your share hit your profit sell price

Woohoo! Congratulations—it's probably time to sell. You've made a profit and it's time to celebrate. If your share has hit your profit sell price (your predetermined price) then I would definitely recommend you sell. Yes, the stock may continue to rise, and you may even wish to get back into it at a later stage, but for now you can safely take your profit.

Sometimes share prices have continued to rise after they hit my profit sell price, but there have also been many that haven't.

I think I bought and sold into Aristocrat Leisure four or five times on its journey upwards. Yes, I would have made more money if I'd held the share for the long term, and that's all well and good in hindsight. There have been many instances where I'm grateful I took the profit when I did as the share price turned back down and I would have lost any profit I'd made.

But here is the exception to this rule. If the share hits your profit sell price a lot more quickly than you expected, then whatever you do, don't sell yet! If a stock is suddenly bursting ahead quickly, then obviously something special is happening with it and if I were you I'd hang on for the ride. There's nothing more frustrating than selling after only two weeks to see the price surge even further ahead in the following weeks when you could have doubled your profit if you'd hung on just a bit longer. This exception, which I call the 'shooting star' phenomenon (not to be confused with the candlestick chart pattern of the same name), is explained in more detail a little further on in this chapter. It's one of the most exciting things about investing (in my opinion) because if you find a 'shooting star' your profit is capable of going crazy and you'll have a dinner party story to impress all your investing friends.

If, however, your share has hit your profit sell price in your expected time frame and has done nothing special to lead you to believe it may surge ahead in the future, then you're perfectly safe in taking your profit now. You might decide to keep holding the stock because there doesn't seem to be anything better around at the moment, but that's your choice—sometimes it pays off, sometimes it doesn't. I'd hate to see you lose all the profit you made simply because you continued to hold too long, but if the company seems stable, then you don't have to sell if it doesn't seem right to you.

Face it, you're probably never going to buy at the cheapest price and sell at the highest price. Even the most successful investors can't make accurate predictions, but by following a plan in which your buy and sell rules are set and easy to follow you have a higher chance of becoming a winner in the market.

Selling because even though the price has increased you don't think it will hit your profit sell price

Sometimes stocks just seem to languish at the same price for ages. If your stock has been sitting at the same price for a while and the time limit you were prepared to hold it for is up, it's time to investigate further. It could be that the share price is just resting before it starts on its uphill spurt again, or it could be due for a correction and be ready to turn down. Looking at a chart might enable you to pinpoint what the case is. Selling now is up to you, and you need to take the following into consideration: are you still happy with the rise, even though it's not as much as you anticipated?

Are you prepared to hold it another few weeks? Is there a better stock that you'd rather invest in? I usually give my shares a bit of breathing room and time to get to the price I want, but if one doesn't reach that price within a reasonable time frame, then I have no qualms about taking the lower price.

After all, a profit is a profit, right? A reasonable time frame for my short-term investments is about three months. If they haven't reached the set profit level by then, and they don't look like getting there in the near future, I sell. You can always get back into the stock at a later date if it decides to resume its climb upwards; in the meantime, it's time to look for better opportunities.

Try to give the price a little leeway too. If the price seems to sit only a few cents away from your sell price, you need to ask yourself whether an extra $30 or $40 is really going to make much difference if you sell now. Sometimes you can wait for a certain price that the share never seems to reach. This tends to happen a lot around certain psychological price points, such as round figures or exact dollar amounts.

Example

Let's say you invest $5000 and you buy your shares at $2.81. From your research you think the price will rise to $3.03 in four or five weeks' time (a gain of about 8 per cent). However, the price seems to hit the $3.00 mark and then just bob around there for quite some time without pushing through. After about eight weeks you figure that it's probably better to take your profit now, even though it's still not at your original profit sell price of $3.03. The profit you do make by selling at $3.00 is $338 instead of $391 if you are able to sell at $3.03. Sometimes a stock will push through a psychological price point quite easily, but other times it won't. Is the extra $53 that you would have gained if you'd waited for the price to rise to $3.03 worth it if it takes another two or three months to get there? Sometimes it's better to take your profit and look for the next big opportunity. You can always get back into this stock if it does push through and begin its journey upwards again.

Selling because the chart is looking bearish or the company has released a negative announcement

A few years back I bought shares in Suncorp Metway as it was looking very good financially. As luck would have it, a few weeks after I'd purchased the shares the CEO quit and the share price fell quite quickly. I actually bought this stock using long-term investing rules so I decided to ride out this glitch (the share price recovered in about six or seven months, thankfully).

If you'd bought according to short-term rules, then this is an example of a good reason to sell. Take your profit because it's likely the price will fall in the weeks following a negative announcement by the company, and you can't afford to just sit around and wait nearly a year to get your money back when investing for the short term. Likewise, by looking at a stock chart you can sometimes tell that the stock is about to turn around. Have a look at Suncorp Group's chart in figure 7.1.

If you're adept at reading charts, there are some clear clues that this stock has moved from bullish in the first half of the chart to bearish from about the beginning of November. The main indication is the number of filled blank candles. I consider more than four filled candles in a row to be very bearish, indicating that it's time to decide whether or not to get out. The other bearish signal is when the price breaks down through the EMA.

If you held this stock, you'd probably consider selling early, even if it hadn't reached your profit sell point.

Reasons to continue holding short-term Investments

You shouldn't sell short-term investments just because you're holding them for the 'short term'. There are two main reasons why I'd continue to hold my short-term investments even if they had increased in price:

$ if they haven't yet reached my profit sell price and the time limit isn't up

$ if they reach my profit sell price within a fortnight of purchase.

Yay! My shares went up!

Figure 7.1: SUN, showing a clear uptrend in the first half, then a slow decline from November

SUNCORP GROUP LTD FPO

Date Range: 1d | 5d | 1m | 3m | **6m** | YTD | 1y | 3y | 5y | 10y | All | Custom

☐ Draw trend lines

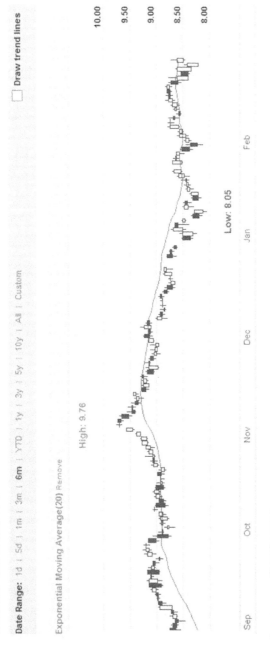

Exponential Moving Average(20) Remove

High: 9.76

Low: 8.05

Source: <www.CommSec.com.au>

The stock hasn't reached the profit sell price and the time limit isn't up

Often, stocks just don't seem to do what you think they will. I've had many stocks that seem to like to tease me by getting really close to my profit sell price and then falling back again to the level where I bought them. While this can be frustrating to watch, if the time limit I set hasn't been reached I continue to hold. It could be a normal movement for a stock to dance around like that so I try to ignore its taunting and wait patiently to see whether it will rise again. Although not every stock I buy reaches my profit sell price, there are many that I've been glad I held because just as I had given up hope they turned around and gave me the profit I was looking for.

If the time limit you set beforehand isn't up then hang in there; it could be one of those annoying stocks that just likes teasing you. Play hard to get and try not to watch it too much; when the time is up you'll be able to decide whether to sell at the lower profit or not.

The stock reaches my profit sell price within a fortnight of purchase

It's likely that during your investing journey you'll stumble upon what I call a 'shooting star', which is a stock that, for whatever reason (and usually I don't know until much later), rises rather dramatically in a short period of time, much more quickly than I'd estimated. Obviously something special is happening with this stock and I don't want to miss out on whatever it is so I continue holding, watching closely to see whether the rise has any chance of slowing down.

When a stock exhibits this behaviour, I usually start to watch its chart very closely for signs that the surge is ending before I consider selling. I usually set a trailing stop loss in this case to help protect the profits that I've made so far because this is the perfect opportunity for taking advantage of this strategy. I'll explain more about the trailing stop loss in chapter 8.

It's also very common during such a price surge for the ASX, or sometimes even ASIC, to ask the company the reason for the sudden increase in price. The company executives usually reply, 'We don't know', which I always find amusing. Someone knows something—there's usually a reason for such increases even if the company itself acts clueless. I don't really care why the share price is increasing, just as long as it is and it takes my money on the ride with it.

Occasionally the ASX or even the company itself will place a trading halt on any further trading activity. This can be nerve wracking, especially if you hold shares in the company, as you aren't allowed to do anything for a few days. An announcement usually precedes the lifting of the halt, which might explain the reason for the increase (although many times it still doesn't explain the increase and you're still left wondering why). After a trading halt is lifted there's usually increased buying and selling of the stock as people scramble to get in or out, depending on the announcement.

The gist of the jargon

ASIC: The Australian Securities & Investments Commission is a regulatory body that keeps track of companies and investors to make sure they are complying with the rules of investing and not doing anything illegal or underhand.

Trading halt: A period of time where all trading on a company is stopped. All buy and sell orders are purged from the market until the halt is lifted. The trading halt can be placed by either the ASX or ASIC, or by the company itself before it puts out a market-sensitive announcement.

This could mean further increases, or a turnaround and decrease in the share price. If the price decreases then you should sell as soon as you can, but if it increases, feel free to hold and enjoy the ride. It's these 'shooting star' stocks that will probably make you the most money in the market. While most of your stocks will make you modest profits or worse, or will do nothing or even decrease in price, every now and then you'll stumble across a 'shooting star' stock and your profits will increase through the roof. Good luck in your search!

Greed versus panic — waiting too long or selling too early

Timing is one of the hardest things to get right when it comes to investing. You're usually either kicking yourself for getting out too soon or wishing you'd jumped ship a lot earlier than you did. There's no doubt that you're probably not going to buy at the cheapest price and sell at the highest price unless you have some sort of crystal ball, so let's dispel that fantasy right away (I've checked many an alternative new-age shop but have yet to find a crystal ball that will tell me which stocks will rise or what the lotto numbers are). So you know that you probably won't sell at the *perfect* time, but how do you know when the *right* time is?

There have been plenty of times when I've held on just that bit too long hoping for a few dollars extra, or celebrated too early and taken my profit and run away only to miss out on an even bigger rise. The only way I'm able to be successful in the market is when I take all emotion out of investing and follow my plan step by step. Think of it as a recipe: miss an ingredient and the end product isn't going to be as tasty. By following a plan, you don't have to rely on how you're feeling to make an investment decision. Can you imagine trying to decide whether to sell if you have the flu, or what to buy after your best friend tells you she's pregnant? Even if you're clear of mind, sometimes just thinking about investing large sums of cash can make even the most rational of us a little crazy.

Greed and panic are two emotions that will ruin your investing goals and must be kept only for Christmas mornings (come on, we all want the biggest gift and start to freak out when the relatives arrive, don't we? Or is that just me?). If it's easier, write your plan down next to the computer or wherever you like to do your research. Then follow your steps one by one. Sometimes it's even helpful to keep a trading diary; that way you can see at a glance why you bought a particular stock and whether you followed the rules properly when buying it. Not every trade will be successful, but believe me you'll be far more successful by following a plan than by trying to buy on instinct.

$ $ $

Having your shares increase in price is one of the most wonderful feelings when it comes to investing in the stock market—it's such a sense of achievement when you've made the right decision and made some money along the way. While it's perfectly fine to feel pride at your accomplishment, it's also time to decide what to do next. Often the biggest mistake a novice investor makes is selling too early for fear that the share price will turn around again, thereby missing out on what the stock was truly capable of. In this chapter, I've tried to explain some different scenarios to help you decide when is the right time to sell, and when you should keep holding the stock. Generally, it will depend on why you bought the stock in the first place: was it a long-term investment, or are you trying to make a quick profit? Looking at each stock individually can usually help you decide whether the profit is reasonable, or something special that should be looked at more closely.

Congratulations on making a successful investment! I wish you many more to come.

Help!
My shares
went down!

Chapter 8

Stocks can be jumpy little critters. One minute they're bouncing high and the next they're falling flat. I'm sure if they were a person you'd classify them as totally insane. But before you start to panic and file for bankruptcy, take a deep breath and follow me.

There's no doubt that it's a scary feeling when your shares go down in price; you immediately think about the money you've lost and tend to forget about the bigger picture. But by now you would have looked at a few charts, and realised that the market never runs in a perfectly smooth line, and that it's very common for a stock (even if it's in an uptrend) to jump up and down quite dramatically. Try not to look at minute-by-minute, hour-by-hour market movements because this will only freak you out more. Very often a share price will decrease before it increases again, as if it's taking a rest before the next big leap.

Don't-panic strategies

Now take a deep breath ... stay calm. Let's look at some don't-panic strategies to help you avoid the anxiety that can occur if your share price falls. Sometimes it's just a matter of being patient and waiting for it to jump back up again, and other times it's time to say goodbye and sell at a loss, so that you can find a better opportunity somewhere else. The good news is that you probably won't lose all of your money if you act quickly. As long as you keep a level head, you should be able to get through any mini-crisis in the market.

Strategy 1: look at the bigger picture

Most stocks are moving all the time. They bounce around every day—sometimes they're up, and sometimes they're down. A small decrease in price is actually very common. Sometimes it seems that the price will rise a bit, then fall back, then rise again. Not every stock will show this behaviour, but you'd be surprised how many do seem to follow this pattern. If you know that a stock may take about six months to a year to rise, then why do you really care what yours did an hour or even a week ago?

I usually try to take in an overall picture of a stock over a period of weeks or months and ignore the everyday fluctuations that can cause even the most stable of us some anxiety. I'm not bothered at all by small movements. The share price can bounce to its heart's content as long as it stays within the rules under which I bought it. There's a point when I say enough is enough, and give it my full attention if it drops too far. That point is at about 10 per cent below what I paid for it. But even then sometimes I'll give it a bit of leeway. If I've bought the stock under long-term investing rules, then it's very likely that I won't even notice it dropping in price because I try to ignore it and only check it every three or so months. I give a lot more attention to my short-term buys, but even then I try not to watch them too much, preferring instead to receive SMS alerts rather than watch the stock intently. And, really, who has the time (or the nerve) to watch a price every five minutes when there's shopping to do, television to watch and socialising to enjoy?

I've already shown you that with long-term investing, stocks generally seem to do well, with most of them moving in a more or less upward direction if you look at them over a decent time period. I'm not saying that every stock will pull through for you if you wait. Some companies will probably never reach the heights they were at in their heyday, but don't let me scare you—there are ways to avoid or at least get out of those stocks early if it comes to that. Generally, if you've done your research, there's a good chance that a small decrease in price is normal and nothing to worry about. But how do you know the difference?

If just looking at the bigger picture is not enough to allay your fears and the stock is truly dropping, then maybe it's time to consider jumping ship.

Strategy 2a: setting a stop loss

Imagine that you could take out an insurance policy on your shares so that if they dropped in price you could get your money back. Ringing your current insurance company and asking for such a policy won't work, but there are strategies you can use to keep your hard-earnt cash from slipping through your fingers before there's nothing left.

The first—and most important—is the stop loss. I can't stress enough how important it is to have a stop loss in place, especially when it comes to short-term investing (see chapter 5 for more on setting stop-loss prices). A stop loss is what nearly all professional investors use to stop losing all their money on a stock. It's a predetermined price point or date you choose beforehand so that if your stock doesn't go as expected you'll take your loss and get out early. While it's not quite as important for long-term investors, I would never buy a share for the short term without setting up a stop-loss plan.

It could be as simple as writing your stop loss on a Post-it note stuck to the side of your computer, or it could be set through your broker to execute automatically at a set price point. I tend not to set up automatic stop losses as I find I sometimes get bumped out when the price just nudges the price I set, but then turns around and returns to a safe level a few moments later. Instead, I've set up a system through my online broker whereby I get an SMS alert on my phone if the share price drops to a certain point. Then I can go online, check what's happening and decide whether I need to get out or not.

As covered in chapter 5, I usually set my stop losses at 10 per cent below the price I paid for the stock. There are exceptions to this rule for certain stocks, but generally I stick with 10 per cent simply because it's a nice round figure and it's about equal to my pain threshold for losing money. I don't usually let it get further than that because then it's more difficult to get my money back.

If your share's price drops 10 per cent, you will need to make 11.1 per cent on your next share to get your money back. If your share's price drops 50 per cent, you'll need to make 100 per cent next time to get back to that level. Now I don't know about your investment skills, but for me making 100 per cent on a stock is a difficult thing to do!

Have a look at table 8.1, which shows how much you'll need to make up to break even if your share decreases in value. As you can see, the earlier you get out, the easier it will be to make your money back. It's important to find out what your threshold is and the amount you'd be prepared to lose. I think

10 per cent is a reasonable figure to set your stop loss at because it's large enough to give your stock a bit of moving room, yet small enough to lose only a tiny portion of your portfolio funds. What are you going to set your stop-loss threshold at?

Table 8.1: breaking even with decreasing share prices

Percentage loss	Percentage you'll need to make back to break even
5%	5.3%
10%	11.1%
15%	17.6%
20%	25.0%
30%	42.9%
35%	53.8%
40%	66.7%
45%	81.8%
50%	100.0%

I actually believe that the key to becoming a successful investor has nothing to do with your ability to choose the right stocks (although that helps), but everything to do with good money-management techniques that include having a stop loss in place. It's been shown that if you pick a bunch of random stocks and invest in them with a stop loss in place so that if they fall you get out quickly, you can still make money in the stock market. Good money management will keep you in the game and make you a successful stock market investor for a lot longer than simply choosing the right stocks to invest in.

In *A Random Walk Down Wall Street* (Reed Business Information, 1996), Burton Malkiel says that 'a blindfolded monkey throwing darts at a newspaper's financial pages could select a portfolio that would do just as well as one carefully selected by experts'.

Basically, even if you choose stocks completely at random, as long as you stick to the rules of cutting your losses early and letting your winners go on to make you money, you'll probably be successful in the market. Malkiel's study goes on to show that the randomly picked stocks often do as well—if not better than—those that have been handpicked, researched and chosen by the professionals.

This theory has been tested in Australia as well (the newspapers always seem to do this by using a dartboard as one of their stock-picker selectors when they run stock competitions), and surprisingly the random stocks or dartboard selections seem to do very well (often better than the professionals!). It makes you wonder why we bother with all that research doesn't it?

So if the key is not so much choosing the right stocks, but practising good money management, just imagine what your returns would look like if you could do both? See? I told you research wouldn't be a waste of time. It can actually help as well.

Strategy 2b: setting a trailing stop loss

I've explained fairly carefully the ordinary stop loss used to help you reduce your losses. Now I'd like to introduce a handy little tip that will help reduce your loss of profit as your share increases in value. A trailing stop loss is merely a price point that moves up as the share price moves up, the theory being that it protects your profits along the way.

Example

Let's say you bought a share for $5.00 and set your first stop loss for 10 per cent below the price you paid—$4.50. After about a month the share price increases to $5.45, so you decide to move your stop loss up to $4.91 (about 10 per cent below $5.45). The next month your share price increases to $6.10 so you move your stop loss to $5.49 (10 per cent below $6.10). Soon after, your shares fall back down to $5.49 and so you sell (since it was your latest stop loss figure).

In this example, you purchased the share for $5.00 and sold for $5.49, representing a profit of 9.1 per cent, which is a very nice little return. Your trailing stop loss kept you from losing the profit you made along the way. If you hadn't moved your stop loss and it had remained at the original figure of $4.50, when the share price decreased even further you'd have lost all the profit you made along the way.

It would have been nicer to sell at the top ($6.10), but let's be realistic here: you never know when the market is going to turn and anyone who tries to predict the share-price top is usually on a wild goose chase. A trailing stop loss can help protect your money when you don't have a clear profit sell target in mind.

I like to amend my stop loss each month for my short-term purchases. If a share is going really well, why would I consider selling it? I'm happy to hang on for the ride and keep amending my stop loss up and up so I can keep the profits along the way.

Strategy 3: cashing out in a bear market

As you know, there are some years when you can't seem to do a thing wrong and the money flows your way, and some years when the market falls around you, taking your money with it—very much like we recently experienced with the GFC. It's almost impossible to avoid a bear market or—worse still—a market crash. (People seem to be able to predict them only in hindsight. I don't know how many 'experts' I've listened to lately who say they knew the market was due for a crash—'Oh yeah, then why did you lose half your money as well, hmm?'). However, if you set up stop losses and get out early enough or take a bigger picture view you could survive a bear market. Even long-term investors who held on for the bumpy ride during previous market slumps have been rewarded. You already know that with long-term investing (10 years or more) the market moves in a generally positive direction. In the market crash of 1987, during which nearly all investors lost a quarter of their portfolio value in one day, the market did start to increase again and by the end of that year the market finished only marginally below where it stood before the crash.

Even now the market has mostly recovered from the latest crash, and it's likely that in the next few years it could rise even further if history has anything to say about it.

But how do you know that you're actually in a bear market or whether it's just a dip in the value of your shares? First off, try to ignore the news reports that are always trying to predict what sort of market we're in; commentators usually get it right only after the fact. It's better to work it out yourself based on how your shares are doing. Usually it's fairly simple to know you're in a bear market — everything is going down in price! The market seems to close lower than it opened more often than not, and pretty soon all your shares hit their stop losses and you sell out. If you do hold a handful of stocks and every one of them hits its stop loss within a few weeks, then it's probably reasonable to assume that you're in a bear market. So what should you do?

My advice here is to sell at your stop losses and stay out of the market for a while. Unless you're proficient at short selling (you sell the share first and then buy it back at a lower price — talk to your broker if you're interested), then it's probably wise just to play it cool until the market turns around. Just keep a watch on the market every few weeks or months until you're confident things have turned back into positive territory. Unless you're willing to ride out the market fluctuations, it might be a good idea to keep your money nice and safe in your bank account (but make sure it has a high interest rate) until prices start to rise again.

This is what I've been doing over the past few years. While I still hold most of my long-term shares, I haven't done any short-term trading for quite some time. Of course, now I'm getting renewed interest in playing for the short term again—it's going to be a fun few years.

Some of the biggest market gains are made by people who buy at the end of a bear market when the prices are cheap (a sale!) and wait until they return to their regular price before selling back to the market, making a nice little profit.

Strategy 4: diversification

You've probably heard the cries from stock market investors everywhere: diversify, diversify and diversify. And yes, it's true that diversification can help smooth out the bumps of the average share portfolio, so if one stock goes down, hopefully the others will go up and help balance things out. But how many stocks should you own in your portfolio for it to be truly diverse?

You need to hold only two different companies for your portfolio to be considered 'diversified', although I like to hold between three and six stocks at any one time. Any less than three and I don't feel completely covered, and any more than six and I can't seem to keep track of them properly, so between three and six stocks works for me. I also try to choose stocks from different sectors. For example, if I hold a stock in the health-care sector, the next stock

I buy might be from the financials or the information technology sector (depending on which sectors are outperforming the market at the time).

The more stocks you hold, the more smoothly your portfolio will move (after all, that's how managed funds work), but it has also been shown that the more stocks you own, the lower the return you'll receive in the long run. In *The Warren Buffett Portfolio* (John Wiley & Sons, 1999), author Robert Hagstrom studied about twelve thousand different portfolios of varying degrees of diversification. Over 10 years the portfolios made the returns shown in table 8.2. The lowest percentage return was that of the portfolio in the study that did the worst, and the highest percentage return was that of the portfolio in the study that did the best.

Table 8.2: results from Hagstrom's study

Stocks held	Lowest percentage return	Highest percentage return
15 stocks	4.4%	26.6%
50 stocks	8.6%	19.2%
100 stocks	10.0%	18.3%
250 stocks	11.5%	16.0%

You can see that the portfolio that held the least number of stocks (15 in this case) had a potential return substantially greater than the highest return for a portfolio of 250 stocks. But you can also see that, while holding 15 stocks showed the potential for the highest per cent return, it also had the potential for the lowest per cent return. This was in contrast to the 250-stocks portfolio, which showed only a marginal difference between the lowest and highest returns in that study.

There's no doubt that diversification will decrease your risks in the sharemarket because your investments are spread across a number of companies. However, you should try to keep the number of stocks you own to a number that you find manageable. There's no point owning more than 50 stocks if you're having trouble keeping track of them all. You'd do better owning a managed fund than trying to do it yourself. Speaking of managed funds …

Strategy 5: investing in managed funds

Perhaps the whole sharemarket ride is too much for you and you'd prefer to sell up and let the professionals do the work instead, so that reading your statement every six months is the only work you have to do. If that's the case, it could be a good idea to look into managed funds (or mutual funds as they're also sometimes called).

This strategy is probably a favourite with lazy girls who really don't want to spend any time doing any sort of research and would rather pay someone to do all the picking and choosing for them.

With as little as $1000 you can buy units in a managed fund with any number of top fund managers. They'll add your money to a pool with others and use that to invest in a large number of different stocks across different sectors, indices or even global markets. Although you don't get any say in what is bought and sold, you can choose from many different types of fund. Some are simple index funds that hold every stock in a certain index, while others might contain only property stocks or international stocks or many other combinations of companies. If you grab a few brochures you'll be amazed at the different types of fund offered.

Despite the fact that fund managers are financial professionals, there's no guarantee they'll make better investment decisions than you would have or even that they'll make a profit at all. However, if you're a nervous person who panics when her shares decrease in price, but still wants to invest in the market, managed funds are a good alternative.

Apart from the obligatory superannuation funds, I don't hold any managed funds myself as I prefer to choose which stocks I buy and sell (and I hate all those fees the managed fund companies charge). Besides, I feel that most managed funds are lacking in challenge and tend to offer only 'mediocre' results. It's better than taking losses, sure, but I like the sense of control over my financial future that choosing my own stocks brings. Of course, this probably comes down to me being a bit of a control freak as well, so I also realise that the stock market isn't for everyone and, as such, a managed fund might suit you better, especially if you twinge at every price decrease.

$ $ $

There's no doubt that seeing your shares decrease in price can be a scary proposition, but if you keep a level head you can ride out the everyday market fluctuations. It's totally normal for a share price to rise and fall many times on its journey. The important feature to look at is the overall direction, ignoring day-to-day fluctuations. The minimum period I look at is weekly movement, but more usually I focus on the monthly movement so that I can ignore the normal fluctuations of a share's price.

Using strategies such as stop losses and diversification can help minimise any losses in the market to improve your return and make you a stock market success. In fact, I consider using stop losses as the single most important strategy that everyone should know about when investing in the stock market. You can also apply other don't-panic strategies such as the trailing stop loss, or diversify your portfolio to minimise losses. It's not the profit that will make you successful; it's your ability to minimise your losses and stay in the game that will make you a winner in the end.

Borrowing to invest

Chapter 9

Do you know that you could buy $100 000 worth of shares with only $30 000 of your own money? That means you'd collect profits on $100 000 worth of shares, dividends on $100 000 worth of shares and only have a small amount of your own money invested. Does this sound too good to be true?

Borrowing money from a bank or financial institution to invest (called a margin loan) is becoming increasingly popular with many investors. You could effectively get access to more shares and make even bigger profits. But be warned! While you can amplify your profits with a margin loan, it also works the other way: you also amplify your losses, making borrowing to invest a risky proposition.

If borrowing to invest is something you've thought about, or even just something you want to know about for future reference, this chapter will guide you through the decision. Ultimately the decision is up to you, but hopefully I can offer help and suggestions along the way.

Should I take out a margin loan?

It may seem that everybody these days is using other people's money (bank loan money) to invest, but this probably doesn't occur as often as you think. Borrowing to invest is far more common for investing in property than it is for investing in shares. So don't even think about doing it just because you think it's what you're supposed to do, or what everybody else is doing.

Taking out a margin loan is not a decision to be made lightly and it's certainly not for the timid. If you're new to the sharemarket or you're not following a sound investment plan that has proven successful for you, then extra money to invest with is not going to help you. In fact, it'll probably put you in a much worse situation.

However, if you've been making good profits by investing over a long period of time, and borrowing is something you've researched carefully and are confident could work for you, it might be time to consider taking out a loan to increase your portfolio. Notice that I say it '*might* be time' and not '*is* time', as taking out a margin loan is not the right choice for some investors even if they're making consistent profits. You'll also need to have built up a substantial cash base of your own money to use (at least $20 000) before a bank will consider lending you money for shares. And as it's a loan, you'll also probably need a secure job because the lender will want to know you're a stable person who can make the interest payments each month whether your shares are doing well or not. Also, it doesn't hurt to have enough excess income to cover the payments if the interest rate increases; you don't want to be struggling because interest on your loan went up an extra 2 per cent.

I personally have never taken out a margin loan, although that's not to say I never will. I'm not opposed to the idea, and once I even withdrew \$15 000 from my credit card to invest in the market. My dear boyfriend nearly had a heart attack when I told him what I'd done, but I felt confident in my abilities and the direction of the stocks I was investing in and luckily it paid off for me. I think there was definitely a bit of luck in that transaction, although I'd been consistently making profits and had a good plan in place, so I wasn't too concerned. But please don't follow my lead. I certainly don't recommend that anyone withdraws money from their credit card to put in the market unless they're absolutely sure of what they're doing. Imagine if things went wrong—you could be in a world of hurt.

Before you make a decision about whether it's a good idea to borrow to invest, have a look at what it could do for you if your shares go up in value, and if your shares go down.

The difference it could make to your bottom line

A margin loan is generally the same as any other loan your bank or financial institution may offer you, but instead of buying a car or a house, you buy shares with the money. Simple in theory, right? Often there are rules that the lending institution puts in place with regard to which stocks you can buy or how much your holdings should be diversified, but you do still have the overall say in what you buy. And as it's a loan, there's still interest to pay.

One benefit of a margin loan is that the interest you pay will probably offer tax benefits. While everyone's individual circumstances are different, in most cases, on any money you borrow that's used for investment purposes, the expenses—such as interest and borrowing fees—can be used to reduce the amount of tax you have to pay. Get in touch with your accountant (every woman has an accountant, right?) and let them work out what tax benefits you'd get to decide whether it's worthwhile in your circumstances before you choose to take out a margin loan.

Now let's get down to actual figures and take a quick look at the sort of return you can get with a margin loan.

Example

Let's say you have a spare $20000 sitting around that you'd like to put in the sharemarket (lucky you, you're loaded!). Generally, lenders will let you borrow up to 70 per cent of the value of the portfolio, so in this instance you could probably borrow $65000 for a total portfolio of $85000. An average interest rate for a margin loan is 8 per cent per annum (check with your bank for its current rates), and for this first example (see table 9.1) we'll imagine that your portfolio has increased in value by 12 per cent for the year.

Table 9.1: portfolio increased in value by 12 per cent

Without margin loan		With margin loan	
Starting capital	$20000	Starting capital	$20000
		Borrowed amount	$65000
		Total portfolio	$85000
Increase of 12%		**Increase of 12%**	
Ending capital	$22400	Ending portfolio	$95200
		Less interest 8%	−$5200
		Less loan	−$65000
		Ending capital	$25000
Profit	$2400	Profit	$5000

You can see that if you had a margin loan your profit would be more than double for the year compared with if you hadn't taken out the loan. You could effectively double or triple your rate of return by taking out a margin loan. Who wouldn't want some extra profit in their hands for no extra work at the end of the year?

But sometimes things aren't this rosy. What would happen if, instead, your portfolio decreased in value over the year, as shown in table 9.2? Let's look at the same example but this time with your portfolio value decreased by 7 per cent.

Table 9.2: portfolio decreased in value by 7 per cent

Without margin loan		With margin loan	
Starting capital	$20000	Starting capital	$20000
		Borrowed amount	$65000
		Total portfolio	$85000
Decrease of 7%		**Decrease of 7%**	
Ending capital	$18600	Ending portfolio	$79050
		Less interest 8%	−$5200
		Less loan	−$65000
		Ending capital	$8850
Profit	−$1400	Profit	−$11150

In this case, you've lost a whopping $11150, when you take into consideration interest on the loan as well as the loss on the portfolio. That's nearly $10000 more than if you hadn't had a loan, and more than half the money you started with; certainly not a good position to be in.

I've kept calculations simple in both these examples and I didn't take into consideration tax benefits or margin calls, but it still gives you an idea of the scale of return or loss you could receive. A margin loan will be of benefit to you only if you can make more than the interest rate you pay. If interest on your loan is charged at 8 per cent per annum, you'd better be making at least 9 per cent per annum in your portfolio; otherwise you're losing money and it's not worth it.

If I haven't scared you off by now and you're still considering applying for a margin loan I bet the next thing you want to know is what's involved in applying for one.

How do I get a margin loan?

Most banks and lending institutions offer some type of margin loan. Usually the lending criteria are very similar to taking out any other sort of loan — there will be paperwork involved and identity checks to perform.

The holdings in your portfolio are usually used to secure the loan and you can add to your own funds or increase the amount borrowed at any time as long as the market value of the portfolio remains within the percentage allowed (the LVR) by the lending institution. If the market value of the portfolio falls below the percentage allowed, your bank might issue a margin call. You'll then be required to deposit more money into the margin account or sell off some of your shares. Usually you only have 24 hours to meet the requirements of your margin call so you'd better have some extra cash lying around or you'll have to sell off a portion of your portfolio. If you don't comply within the set time period, it's possible that your lender will sell your investments without your go-ahead, so it's important to monitor your account and act quickly when necessary before this happens.

> **The gist of the jargon**
>
> **LVR:** Loan-to-valuation ratio. The percentage of the market value of the approved shares that a lending institution is prepared to lend against.

To avoid getting caught with a margin call you might consider borrowing less than the allowed LVR so that you have some breathing room if your shares do decrease in price.

> **The gist of the jargon**
>
> **Margin call:** When the value of your portfolio decreases to below the allowed lending limit of your margin loan, the bank or financial institution might issue a margin call and ask you to deposit additional funds so that the account is returned to the allowed LVR.

Each margin loan has a different set of rules, so make sure you understand yours completely before you sign on the dotted line. You'll need to check things such as:

$ *Minimum loan balance.* Some lenders require you to pay interest on the minimum loan balance even though you may have borrowed less, or paid some of the loan back early. Make sure you won't be slugged with interest payments on money you haven't actually borrowed.

$ *Paying the loan back.* Is it possible to pay the loan back early, or prepay your interest payments? Sometimes lenders charge you a fee for early repayment of a loan, or even specify that prepaid interest is non-refundable. Make sure your deal is something you're comfortable with.

§ *Margin call buffer.* Is a buffer offered by the lender (say 5 per cent) if your shares decrease to below the allowed LVR? It could be worthwhile trying to negotiate a buffer so that your shares have a bit more room to move.

How much should I borrow?

Well, that's entirely up to you, but I'd recommend you borrow below your allowed LVR so that there's less likelihood of a margin call. If your loan-to-valuation ratio is 70 per cent and you borrow to the full amount, your investments only have to decrease by 6.7 per cent in value before a margin call will be issued. Since share prices could easily fall by this small amount, it's likely that you'll be asked to cough up more cash or sell some securities in this case. Many lenders recommend you borrow only up to 50 per cent of the value of your shares to offset any risks of a margin call. If you borrowed only 50 per cent and your LVR was 70 per cent, your shares would have to decrease by 33 per cent in value before you were issued a margin call. This is a much safer level to be at, because usually you wouldn't let your shares fall by this amount if you had a stop-loss strategy in place.

Table 9.3 (overleaf) shows how much your investments would have to fall with different borrowing levels if you borrowed from a lender with an LVR of 70 per cent. As you can see, borrowing less than the allowed LVR will significantly decrease your risk of getting a margin call, and is definitely recommended if you choose to take out a margin loan.

Using the equity in your home

Another method of borrowing to invest that seems to be gaining popularity is using the equity from your home loan to invest in the stock market. This method only applies to homeowners with either a line-of-credit loan or a loan with a substantial chunk of money already paid off that they can borrow back.

Table 9.3: borrowing from a lender with an LVR of 70 per cent

How much you borrowed (%)	Margin call if share prices decrease (%)
70 (full LVR)	6.7
60	20.0
50	33.3
40	46.7
30	60.0
20	73.3
10	86.7

Using the equity in your home is an alternative to applying for a margin loan as the interest rate on a home loan is usually a lot cheaper and you won't be at risk of a margin call. Even so, the thought that you could potentially be putting your home at risk is enough to deter many people from using this method.

Example

Let's say you have a line-of-credit loan for your house and you've paid down $70 000 over the past few years (so you could potentially use the equity if you wanted to). I'll use the same figures as I did with the margin loan so that you can see the difference. I've used a lower interest rate, which was standard for home loans at the time of writing.

Table 9.4 shows where your shares increased in value. You're nearly $1000 better off than in the margin-loan example due simply to lower interest on the loan.

Table 9.4: increase in share value

Without loan		With loan	
Starting capital	$20000	Starting capital	$20000
		Borrowed amount	$65000
		Total portfolio	$85000
Increase of 12%		**Increase of 12%**	
Ending capital	$22400	Ending portfolio	$95200
		Less interest 6.5%	−$4225
		Less loan	−$65 000
		Ending capital	$25975
Profit	$2400	Profit	$5975

Table 9.5 is the scary example where your shares decrease in value.

Table 9.5: decrease in share value

Without loan		With loan	
Starting capital	$20000	Starting capital	$20000
		Borrowed amount	$65000
		Total portfolio	$85000
Decrease of 7%		**Decrease of 7%**	
Ending capital	$18600	Ending portfolio	$79050
		Less interest 6.5%	−$4225
		Less loan	−$65000
		Ending capital	$9825
Profit	−$1400	Profit	−$10175

Again, you're slightly better off due to the lower interest on the loan. However, it will probably mean that you've got a few more years of saving to make up that $10 000 you lost in the market (or a few more years paying off your home loan if you want to use the loss this way). Your home probably won't be at risk unless you lose all the money and your job as well so that you can't make your repayments; but, when you borrow to invest — a loss in the stock market, even with the lower interest rate — means that you stand to lose a lot of money.

$ $ $

There can be some great benefits to a margin loan:

$ the tax benefits of claiming the interest or fees charged

$ being able to diversify your portfolio because you have more funds to spread over more stocks

$ the increased leverage of using those funds to increase your returns.

However, you could experience huge losses if your portfolio decreases in value — not only will you have lost money on your shares, you'll still have to pay the interest on the loan. If you're consistently making profits in the market and have a sound investment plan in place, then it could be something that will work for you and increase your profits. If you decide this is something you want to look into further, it's worthwhile shopping around for the best deal or talking to a financial planner or accountant about whether it could be tax effective for you.

Options, warrants and futures

Chapter 10

As you get further into investing and more comfortable with buying and selling you'll no doubt come across options and other leveraged securities such as warrants and futures. Options in particular are very popular right now as, even though they're risky, they can effectively multiply your results, creating bundles of money very quickly — anything that promises a high return is attractive to most people.

But options are certainly not for everyone. They're risky. While you can make a lot of money quickly, the opposite is also true and you can lose your money just as fast. But once you're willing to give them a go and are fully aware of the risks, options can be a very useful strategy for the experienced short-term investor. So what exactly are they and what sort of results can be achieved by trading them?

Keeping your options open

Naked call, put option, covered call — they all sound weird, huh? (I still giggle every time I hear the term 'naked call'). By the end of this chapter you'll have a clearer understanding of what they are and how to trade them.

But first, what exactly is an option? Basically it's a right, but not an obligation, whereby you get to buy (or sell) a stock at a specified price in the future.

I'll use a shopping analogy to help make it clearer. Say there's a great pair of shoes, but they're so hot right now you suspect they might be more expensive in a month's time when you need them for that swanky party (okay, so most analogies don't bear close examination). Instead of buying them now, you make a deal with the shopkeeper—you might want to buy the shoes in a month's time at an agreed price. You pay a small fee (deposit) for the privilege of making this deal. At the end of the month, you go in and decide whether you still want them. If they've gone up in price, then you're able to buy them at the cheaper price that you agreed on beforehand. If they're now on sale, you don't have to buy them at all (you'd probably buy them on sale instead) although the shopkeeper still gets to keep the fee (deposit) you paid upfront. So it's sort of a win–win situation. If the shoes went up in price, you get to buy them at the cheaper price, but if they went down in price, you don't have to do anything or you could buy them at the cheaper price if you still wanted to. It's exactly the same concept with share options. In fact, the only cost to you (if the share goes against you) is the fee you've spent for the right to buy (or sell) the option.

The most common way of trading in options is to buy an option contract that someone else has written. You'll pay a small fee (a premium) for that privilege and before the end of the date specified you either exercise that option or leave it to expire. Alternatively, you might have no interest in the share itself but want to trade the option (re-sell it to someone else) for profit. One option contract is generally for 1000 shares in that company. The two simplest options are the call option and the put option.

Call option

A call option is what happened in our shoe example. You think the price will go up, so you lock in a specified price for a period of time. If the price does go up you get to buy at the cheaper price and you make money. If it goes down you do nothing. Let's say you're interested in buying an option over BHP. It's currently trading at $46.64 and you're interested in buying an option because you think the price will go up. Figure 10.1 on p. 179 shows some options listed on the ASX that you've found are available for BHP right now. To decipher the jargon used in figure 10.1:

$ *Code* is simply the name of the option. It includes the three-letter stock code (in this case BHP), then a two- (or more) number/letter combination that identifies the particular option contract.

$ *Expiry* is the date when the option will expire.

$ *P/C* identifies the type of option (call or put).

$ *Exercise* is the price at which the buyer gets to buy the shares if they exercise the option. The lower the exercise price the more expensive the option is (as the exercise price increases, the bid and offer prices decrease).

$ *Bid* and *offer* are the prices at which people are prepared to buy and sell the option, just as with normal shares. If any price has a T next to it, it's because there was no valid market quote at the time, so the ASX has calculated a theoretical price.

177

$ *Last* is the last traded price of the option and when it was last traded (date and/or time). The cheaper the option price, the higher the exercise price.

$ *Volume* is the number of contracts traded so far. For this example, BHPZ88 is the most popular option of those listed.

$ *Open interest* is the number of outstanding contracts available to be bought.

You've decided that BHP is very likely to get up past $47.00 by the end of January and you'd like to buy a call option contract instead of buying the stock outright in case you're wrong.

You look at the following three options contracts (I've used the offer price as the price you pay, although it's possible you might get it more cheaply than this).

$ BHPPU7: one contract of 1000 shares at 0.675 = $675 for a strike price of $47.00.

$ BHPZ88: one contract of 1000 shares at 0.300 = $300 for a strike price of $48.00.

$ BHPPV7: one contract of 1000 shares at 0.110 = $110 for a strike price of $49.00.

You'll notice that the prices for the options get cheaper the further away from the actual price they get.

You decide that BHPPV7, while cheaper than the others, has a strike price that's a little too optimistic for your calculations so you discard it. You also think that BHPPU7 is a bit too expensive, and you finally choose to purchase one contract of BHPZ88—just right, as Goldilocks would say.

Figure 10.1: some of the call options on BHP as listed on the ASX

Shares

Code	Last	$ +/-	Bid	Offer	Open	High	Low	Volume	Options	Warrants & Structured Products	CFDs	Chart	Status
BHP*	46.650 ˅	-0.600	46.650	46.660	46.710	46.850	45.600	9,826,859	Options	Warrants & Structured Products	CFDs	⟋	XD XQ

Options (Show Open Interest only)

Code	Expiry date	P/C	Exercise	Bid	Offer	Last	Volume	Open interest	Margin Price
BHPIK9	24/03/2011	Call	45.500	1.570	1.675	0.000		786	1.785
BHPVT7	24/03/2011	Call	45.510	1.550	1.680	1.715	7	555	1.740
BHPZS8	24/03/2011	Call	46.000	1.230	1.280	0.000		2.004	1.385
BHPPX7	24/03/2011	Call	46.010	1.205	1.270	1.280	7	327	1.340
BHPP17	24/03/2011	Call	46.500	0.900	0.950	0.990	20	2.230	1.030
BHPVW7	24/03/2011	Call	46.510	0.875	0.940	0.000		166	1.030
BHPPU7	24/03/2011	Call	47.000	0.625	0.675	0.680	130	3.237	0.730
BHPQ17	24/03/2011	Call	47.010	0.605	0.665	0.000		324	0.720
BHPUA7	24/03/2011	Call	47.500	0.415	0.455	0.440	35	2.028	0.500
BHPZL7	24/03/2011	Call	47.510	0.505	0.505	0.000		30	0.510
BHPZ88	24/03/2011	Call	48.000	0.240	0.300	0.270	188	3.617	0.325
BHPZP7	24/03/2011	Call	48.010	0.340	0.340	0.000		126	0.350
BHPCX8	24/03/2011	Call	48.500	0.160	0.190	0.175	14	806	0.200
BHPPV7	24/03/2011	Call	49.000	0.100	0.110	0.110	24	2.702	0.135
BHPZS7	24/03/2011	Call	49.010	0.140	0.140	0.000		20	0.145

Example: purchasing one contract of BHPZ88

One option contract for BHP at a strike price of $48.00
Cost to you: $300 plus any brokerage costs

Let's say you were correct and a week later the share price had indeed increased and was now trading at $49.01. You now have two choices: you could sell the option, or exercise it now or closer to the exercise date.

Example: profit if you exercise the option

Purchase: 1000 × $48.00 = $48 000
Sell: 1000 × $49.01 (the current trading price) = $49 010
Profit: 49 010 − 48 000 = $1010 profit less cost of option ($300) = $710

In this case you made a profit of $710. Even if you don't have the $48 000 lying around to purchase the shares, you can still receive this. You usually have three business days after the day of trade to settle your transaction, which means if you buy and sell within that time period (and you would probably sell straightaway to realise your profit) you don't actually need to cough up the cash—the difference will simply be deposited into your account on the settlement day.

If you had chosen instead to re-sell the call (called 'closing out'), then it's likely the price of the option would have increased because the price of the share has increased and you could realise your profit that way. In the next example, we'll imagine that the option is now worth $1.00.

Example: profit if you close out the option

Purchase: 1000 × 0.300 = $300

Sell: 1000 × 1.000 = $1000

Profit: $700 less any brokerage costs

If, however, you were incorrect and the share price went down, you'd have lost $300 (the cost of the option).

Put option

Put options are similar to call options except that when you think the price will go down, you buy a put, which gives you the option to sell the shares at a certain price (even if you don't own them yet). A typical list of put option prices is shown in figure 10.2 (overleaf).

If the share price does go down, you buy at the low price and sell at the higher price you agreed beforehand in the put, hence making a profit. If the share goes up instead, you do nothing. Buying a put looks very much like buying a call. The only difference is that this contract gives you the right to sell the shares at the specified time rather than buy them.

Both of the put and call options I've described assume you're buying options that someone else has written, but you can write them yourself too.

Writing options

You can write either call options or put options, and sometimes you don't even need to own the shares.

Writing call options

You have two options when writing a call option: either the covered call (where you own the shares) or the naked call (where you don't).

Figure 10.2: some of the put options on BHP as listed on the ASX

Shares

Code	Last	$ +/-	Bid	Offer	Open	High	Low	Volume	Options	CFDs	Chart	Status
BHP*	46.650 ⌄	-0.600	46.650	46.660	46.710	46.850	46.600	9,826,859	Options	CFDs	⋈	XQ XQ

Options (Show Open Interest only)

Code	Expiry date	P/C	Exercise	Bid	Offer	Last		Volume	Open Interest		Margin Price
BHPKU7	28/04/2011	Put	43.000	0.255	0.255	0.000			394		0.270
BHPLC7	28/04/2011	Put	43.500	0.315	0.355	0.000			380		0.335
BHPEW8	28/04/2011	Put	43.510	0.270	0.270	0.000			8		0.265
BHPLU7	28/04/2011	Put	44.000	0.365	0.000	0.380		1	330		0.405
BHPLX7	28/04/2011	Put	44.500	0.480	0.520	0.485		13	144		0.495
BHPWU7	28/04/2011	Put	44.510	0.460	0.460	0.000			5		0.460
BHPP87	28/04/2011	Put	45.000	0.585	0.635	0.590		11	735		0.605
BHPFT8	28/04/2011	PLt	45.010	0.000	0.000	0.605		1	8		0.585
BHPP47	28/04/2011	Put	45.500	0.720	0.770	0.000			720		0.730
BHPFU8	28/04/2011	Put	45.510	0.690	0.815	0.000			3		0.715
BHPMU7	28/04/2011	Put	46.000	0.875	0.910	0.885		125	1,289		0.880
BHPCW8	28/04/2011	Put	46.010	0.860	0.930	0.860		3	4		0.855
BHPP67	28/04/2011	Put	46.500	1.065	1.125	0.000			492		1.055
BHPTQ7	28/04/2011	Put	47.000	1.280	1.345	1.265		1	151		1.255
BHPUD7	28/04/2011	Put	47.500	1.535	1.600	0.000			77		1.495

Covered call

The covered call is the most common way of writing options and the one most people are familiar with. Let's say you own 1000 ANZ shares that you're prepared to sell. You're entitled to write one contract (an option contract is usually 1000 shares) in which you will agree to sell those shares to someone else (whoever is buying the option) at a certain price and time in the future (set by you).

The buyer will pay you a fee (deposit) for that right. If the time limit arrives and the buyer exercises the option, you have to sell them to the buyer at the price you set, no matter what the price in the market is. You'll get to keep both the fee they paid you and the profit (if you made a profit) that you sold your shares for.

If the buyer doesn't exercise the option, you get to keep the fee and the shares.

Naked call

The other way of writing an option is the naked call, where you don't actually own the shares you're agreeing to sell. In this case you're hoping that the price in the market drops so that the buyer doesn't exercise the option and you get to keep the fee they paid you, but you don't have to cough up the shares. If, however, the market moves against you and the shares rise in price, the buyer will probably exercise the option at the lower price, in which case you'll have to buy them before you can sell them. Obviously you'll have to buy at market prices, which will be higher than the price you agree to sell them at and you'll make a loss. Oh well, at least you get to keep the fee they paid you.

Writing put options

Writing a put option means that you want to buy shares at a specified price and are prepared to offer a contract for that right.

As such, you'd be of the opinion that the market is either trending sideways or about to turn up, and the buyer is of the opinion that it will go down. If the shares do go up in price, the buyer will likely not exercise the option, and you get to keep the fee. Be warned—if the shares decrease in price it's likely that the buyer will exercise the option and force you to purchase the shares at the lower price. Again, while you'll get to keep the fee for writing the option, you could be facing a big loss if the price goes against you.

The gist of the jargon

Covered call: You own the shares and write an option to sell them at a predetermined price in the future.

Naked call: You don't own the shares but still write an option to sell them at a predetermined price in the future. As you can imagine, this can be risky, and it's not called a naked call for nothing—lots of people have lost the shirt off their back this way.

Unless you have experience in options and have defensive actions in place, it's advisable to only buy exchange-traded options or write covered calls until you gain more experience. While you can make fast money with shares, you can also lose it just as quickly.

Multiply your results with warrants and futures

Like options, warrants and futures are contracts to buy or sell a particular asset on a specified date. The ASX currently trades futures on selected stock market indices, commodities (grain and wool) and electricity. You can also trade international futures over a wide range of assets including interest rates, gold and currencies. Many farmers trade futures over their commodities to help lock in a price for their product.

Warrants, on the other hand, are contracts issued from a financial institution (such as a bank) over a particular share or sector. While warrants are similar to options in that they're contracts over particular shares, you can only ever buy warrants (not write them) as they're written exclusively by financial institutions and not by regular stockholders. There could be call or put warrants and, like options, if you buy a call warrant you're expecting the related share price to increase, and if you buy a put warrant you're expecting the price to fall.

Figure 10.3 (overleaf) shows a typical warrant list. Note that *ratio* refers to the number of warrants required to be exercised in order to receive one share in the underlying stock.

You'll need to get a special trading account from your broker to be allowed to trade warrants or futures (and sometimes even for trading options), so check whether you can gain access before delving into these leveraged securities.

You can find the full list of options and warrants on the ASX website at <www.asx.com.au/asx/markets/equityPrices.do> under the tabs 'Options' and 'Warrants/Structured Products' respectively.

$ $ $

I'm yet to really get into trading options or warrants, but I know many people who have used them successfully. They can provide an extra income for your portfolio and reap returns that you wouldn't believe possible.

If options and other leveraged securities are of interest to you, check out the free online courses run by the ASX or check out your bookstore for some great books that include strategies to help you achieve success in this area.

Figure 10.3: a typical list of some of the warrants for the stock code CBA for May 2011

Warrants & Structured Products prices

Shares

Code	Last	$ +/-	Bid	Offer	Open	High	Low	Volume	Options	Warrants & Structured Products	CFDs	Chart	Status	Announcements
CBA *	51.560	-0.130	51.550	51.560	51.300	51.690	51.280	842.486	Options	Warrants & Structured Products	CFDs	✎	XD	Recent

Warrants & Structured Products

Code	Type	Expiry	Exercise	Ratio	Bid	Offer	Last	Volume	Valuation	Offer doc.	Status
CBAIOV	Call	26/05/2011	42.500	1	10.010	10.020	0.000	0	10.100	🗎	XD
CBAIOL	Call	26/05/2011	45.000	1	8.290	8.300	12.470	0	8.370	🗎	XD
CBAXOB	Call	26/05/2011	48.000	4	1.095	1.105	1.395	0	1.120	🗎	
CBAXOC	Call	26/05/2011	50.000	4	0.590	0.600	0.600	0	0.620	🗎	
CBAWOA	Call	26/05/2011	51.000	5	0.650	0.655	0.665	0	0.665	🗎	
CBAXOD	Call	26/05/2011	51.000	4	0.280	0.290	0.360	0	0.310	🗎	
CBAXOA	Call	26/05/2011	51.500	4	0.000	0.000	0.240	0	0.001	🗎	
CBAXOE	Call	26/05/2011	52.000	4	0.000	0.000	0.355	0	0.245	🗎	
CBAWOB	Call	26/05/2011	54.000	5	0.355	0.360	0.425	0	0.365	🗎	
CBAVZK *	Call	26/05/2011	56.000	4	0.120	0.130	0.165	0	0.125	🗎	

Further study

Chapter 11

Hopefully you've grasped the basics that I've outlined; you may even have the investing bug and want to learn more. Luckily for you we live in a time of wonderfully accessible information. At the end of a modem you can find a whole plethora of strategies, rules and concepts. Hundreds of books and seminars all seem to claim that they have the best way to make money in shares. Even your cab driver can probably offer words of wisdom when it comes to investing in the sharemarket. It can be quite overwhelming!

However, if your cab driver starts giving you stock tips, perhaps it's time to consider getting out of that company, if you own shares in it, because it may be oversaturated. Too many cooks really can spoil the broth — or the share price in this case.

Investing is an ongoing learning process. No matter how much you know there always seems to be something new to learn and discover. I still like to learn new techniques and find out how other people invest. While I hope I've given you some great tools to get started with investing in shares, you can go forward and learn more, and I encourage you to do so. There are some wonderful resources available to help you on your journey. Whether you prefer learning at your own pace or like the structure of a class, plenty of information is available.

Investment books

Have you checked out the finance section in your local bookshop recently? (Of course you have, since it was probably the section where you found my book.) There are literally hundreds of books on finance ranging from beginner's level to advanced, on topics from writing a budget to investing in everything from property to shares to whatever else is hot at the moment.

I'm a book person. I love reading about how other people have used different strategies to become successful in the stock market. I also like being able to learn things at my own pace, skipping sections if I'm not interested and returning to chapters I want to re-read. In fact, nearly everything I've learned about the stock market I acquired from books, adapting the strategies to fit my own style. Not everything I read was helpful, nor do I use the majority of it, but that's because I like to keep things simple and many books out there just seem far too complicated for my liking. However, I don't regret a thing I've learned along the way as I believe all knowledge will make me a better investor.

Here I've listed some of my favourite books. Some are those that got me started on the investing road, and others I've purchased along the way. I still refer to most of them today. I hope you'll find them just as useful as I did.

Buffettology

Mary Buffett (Fireside, 1997)

This was the very first book that got me interested in investing in the stock market. If the master Warren Buffett uses these methods, then it's good enough for me. Many of my rules of long-term investing have been adapted from the principles in this book. I also liked reading the stories about how Buffett acted towards his family (especially one Christmas Day).

Discover the Wealth Within You

Ric Edelman (Harper Business, 2002)

This book is broken down into two main sections. I liked the first section on goal setting—the author's main point is that investing for a purpose like saving for a holiday or house is a much stronger motivator than simply investing for the sake of it. While he mainly talks about managed funds instead of direct investing, his principles are nonetheless sound.

How I Made $2 000 000 in the Stock Market

Nicolas Darvas (Lyle Stuart, 1986)

This is a book I think every investor should own. It's a very interesting story about how Darvas made millions in the stock market by using a simple box theory. While the Darvas box method didn't exactly work for me, his idea that if the price fell through the bottom of the box he would sell is very similar to the cutting-your-losses strategy that most investors use.

How to Think Like Benjamin Graham and Invest Like Warren Buffett

Lawrence A. Cunningham (McGraw-Hill, 2001)

More involved strategies of Warren Buffett. Benjamin Graham was the guy to whom Buffett attributes his successful investing method. This book is much heavier going than the other Buffett book I own, but if you can get past all the efficient market theory analogies, you might gain a lot of information on value investing.

Ordinary People, Extraordinary Wealth

Rick Edelman (Harper Business, 2000)

This book shows that it's usually the people next door who are making the big dollars and not the pompous guy in a business suit. It also goes to prove that you don't need to be making hundreds of dollars to become rich; even low income earners are able to acquire wealth with a good investment plan.

Rich Dad Poor Dad

Robert T. Kiyosaki (TechPress, 1997)

This is another all-time classic finance book. While it's more a 'why' book than a 'how' book, it's still interesting to know that all it takes is a change in thinking for anyone to become rich.

Secrets for Profiting in Bull and Bear Markets

Stan Weinstein (McGraw-Hill, 1988)

Weinstein shows easy ways to spot bull and bear markets and to analyse when shares are ready to break out of their current trends. He describes shares as being in one of four distinct phases: either at the bottom, increasing in price, at the top or decreasing in price. He shows you how to recognise each stage and profit accordingly.

The Successful Investor

William J. O'Neil (McGraw-Hill, 2004)

I really liked O'Neil's money-management techniques. While his methods for choosing shares are based on US stocks, they still have great value for buying Australian shares. I've adapted a few of his principles to my short-term strategies. His website has a lot of free information on investing and is worth a visit even if you don't invest in US stocks.

Top Stocks

Martin Roth (Wrightbooks—published annually)

If you want to decrease the amount of time you spend researching companies, get this book as it's all done for you. This annual publication is worth every cent. It lists about one hundred stocks, all of which have been vetted to discard those with high debt ratios or low return-on-equity figures. If you want to invest for the long term, then this book is highly recommended for cutting down your research time.

Trading Secrets, 2nd edition

Louise Bedford (Wrightbooks, 2005)

A great guide to short-term trading. Bedford's book got me interested in short-term trading and candlestick charting; I credit her for opening my eyes to the fact that long-term investing wasn't the only way to invest.

Money Makeover

Vanessa Rowsthorn and Nina Dubecki <www.moneygirl.com.au> (Wrightbooks, 2010)

A good general finance guide that covers the basics of saving money and investing. Has some great tips on how to factor life's changes—such as having babies, changing relationships or changing (or leaving) your job—into your finances.

Classes and courses

Maybe you'd prefer the social contact and structure of a class or course. Classes and courses can be helpful for grasping new techniques and strategies as someone is there to teach the concepts to you and explain ideas further if you don't understand them straightaway. There are many great classes and courses run by different companies that are worth looking into. You could attend a one-off seminar or class to give you information on a new investment style, or you could take a course over a period of weeks or months. Alternatively, if you don't have the time to attend such events, the ASX website has a selection of online courses ranging from beginner to advanced level that you can take at any time, at your own pace, for free, just by signing up to their website. The ASX also runs lunchtime seminars and presentations that you can attend for a small fee.

One note of caution: please make sure you check out the company that's running the course or seminar first, as some courses can be extremely expensive and sometimes the company may have been involved in dodgy dealings. It pays to do some research before you enrol. I'm not saying that all expensive courses are a waste of money; some of them are invaluable and you'll make the cost back tenfold with what you learn. Others just repeat information you can get elsewhere in books or online, so make sure you're getting a fair deal—I would hate any of you to get involved in the latest scam. As a general rule of thumb, if they're offering a free seminar that's really just a sales pitch for a much more expensive seminar, it's worth giving it a miss. Ditto that if you ask a question and they don't give a straightforward answer.

Generally, you'd expect to pay no more than a few hundred dollars (or less) for a really good seminar. If they're asking for thousands of dollars, you know that the only people getting rich are the people running it, and they don't really care about the attendees.

Not too long ago, I saw an investment seminar on day trading advertised with an entry price of $15 000 claiming it could make you a millionaire with its secret strategies. Are you kidding me!? Run, run, run as fast as you can from scams like that.

The internet

The internet can be invaluable when it comes to infor-mation—especially for research. You can find out nearly everything you'd like to know about the company you're thinking of investing in: its profits and losses for the past years, who its directors are and what it actually does (this is very important to know—that three-letter stock code does actually represent a real company that runs some sort of business!).

You can also search for strategies and techniques other people have used—some of which may work for you, many of which won't—and you can visit chat rooms or forums to discuss investing techniques with others. However, I recommend that you try to avoid taking any tips offered—by the time someone offers you a stock tip on a forum it's usually a losing bet. I've already mentioned how easy it is to place your buy and sell orders online, or even just to find the current price of a share at any time of the day.

However, as good as the internet can be for research, it can also steer you in the wrong direction or, even worse, you might get lured into someone's get-rich-quick website thinking you're following some legitimate advice. A good rule of thumb is that if someone wants you to pay for information or buy a special ebook for $97 that will give you the secrets to trading (because it just made them $100000 overnight using these 'undisclosed' techniques), then please close your browser window fast because it's probably not going to make you rich. The old saying goes that the only person getting rich from a $97 ebook is the person selling it—not the person buying it.

Anyway, you can usually get much better advice from buying real books (like this one) for less than $30 or even less than $10 if you own an electronic reading device such as Kindle.

Investment clubs

Maybe you'd like the social aspect of joining a club? Investment clubs, where groups of people get together to learn about the stock market and make investment decisions for the group, are gaining in popularity. Usually the decisions about what to invest in are made by democratic polls of the members so you won't get an individual say in what you buy and sell, but it's a great way to be surrounded by like-minded people.

A now famous investment club was the Beardstown Ladies Investment Club. Its members were 14 elderly women who boasted an impressive average return of 23.4 per cent per annum in the 10 years they were trading up to 1993. Unfortunately, the members had miscalculated their return, and after an audit it was found they had only earned an average of 9.1 per cent per annum during that period. As you would imagine the members were understandably shocked at their miscalculation.

This brings me to an interesting point about investment clubs. I think the main benefit of them is that you can learn about researching, planning investment strategies, and buying and selling shares in a group environment and have some fun along the way. But nobody has ever grown rich in an investment club, as risky strategies are usually voted out in favour of safer methods. Research has shown that such clubs often perform below the index.

If you'd like to join a group or start your own, both the Australian Securities & Investments Commission and the Australian Securities Exchange websites have information about setting one up.

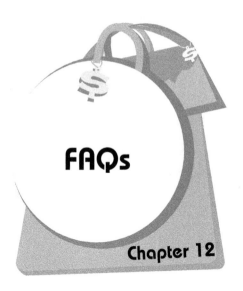

FAQs

Chapter 12

Since the first edition of *Shopping for Shares* came out — and even before that — a lot of people have asked me questions about the stock market and very often I shrug while admitting that I don't know the answers. Yes, I guiltily admit that it's true — I *still* don't know everything there is to know about investing in shares. And yet I still make a profit — how is that possible?

I think the key is something my mum used to always say to me and that was to keep things simple. If you try to overcomplicate things, then more can go wrong. And of course, given my busy lifestyle, I don't really have time for (nor do I care about) complicated strategies or earnings forecasts.

Really, just show me a company with good financials or one that's rising in price and I'm happy enough.

However, that's not to say that I don't know *anything*. I think if you've read this book you'll know I have some idea of what I'm talking about, so I decided to list some of the questions I get asked most frequently and that I actually do know the answer to or have an opinion about.

So here they are: a few of the most asked questions.

Should I buy penny stocks?

This is the most common question I'm asked. People want to know whether buying penny stocks — or stocks that are valued at just one cent — is a good idea.

You'll often find 'get-rich-quick' salespeople telling you that penny stocks are a winning investment strategy. Particularly for people who don't have a lot of money to invest in the market, and on the surface it does seem like a worthwhile strategy.

Many of these companies only have to increase by one cent and you've automatically doubled your money. In fact, sometimes they only have to increase by half a cent and you've made a huge profit. You'll often find that companies that trade at such low prices trade by one-tenth of a cent or less as well. So it could be that your company starts at 0.015 cents and finishes at 0.017 cents. Any low-valued stocks are usually classified as penny stocks — even those that are valued at 10 cents or more — because they're so low that even a small increment in price is enough to ensure big profits.

Now let's look at the theory behind this strategy. Say you find a company that's currently trading at 0.023 cents and you decide to purchase $5000 worth of shares in that company. The company only has to increase by one measly cent and you'll have made almost a 50 per cent return on your money.

Example

Buy $5000 worth of shares at 0.023 cents per share = 217 391 shares (Sounds like an impressive number of shares to hold, doesn't it?)

Sell 217391 shares at 0.033 cents = $7173.90

With most shares it only takes a few days or weeks for them to rise by one cent, so you could make a quick few thousand every week by buying in and out of the stock as it rises and falls. If your company falls again to 0.023 cents the following week you can buy back into it with the $7173.90 you now have.

Example

Buy $7173 worth of shares at 0.023 cents per share = 311869 shares
Sell 311869 shares at 0.033 cents = $10291.67

If the share continues to make small movements, you can keep buying back in every time it falls to 0.023 and sell again at 0.033. Continue to do this a few times and you can see that there's some massive money to be made.

Does this sound like the best investment strategy you've ever heard of, or does it sound too good to be true? The truth is that while this concept looks awesome on paper, it's rarely quite as good as it appears to be and many people who buy into cheap stocks get burned very quickly. I'll tell you why.

For starters, it can be quite difficult to find cheap stocks. They're usually way outside the top 500 companies (although there are a few in the All Ords too) and as you would expect, they don't fit any of the rules that I'd normally follow. At the time of writing, in the All Ords there are only 15 or so companies trading at less than 10 cents, and only one that is at the magic one cent mark. You'll find that just as fast as you can make money, you can also lose it.

Most of these companies are quite illiquid, meaning that there aren't high levels of trading taking place within them. So even if you want to sell at a higher price, very often no-one wants to buy at that price. And even if they do, trying to move such large numbers in one hit is very likely to affect the share price mid transaction. You might be able to only sell one-half or one-third of your holdings until you wait patiently for another buyer to want to purchase at your agreed level.

And of course, very often the company falls so low that it gets into financial trouble and there's a very real possibility that the company could dissolve, taking all your money with it.

Let's look at a real-life example: Crescent Gold (CRE). As you can see in figure 12.1 (overleaf), Crescent Gold has reached a high of 13 cents and a low of 5 cents. While there's quite a bit of difference between those two price points, it's also clear that this company is in a downward trend.

What's most clear are two different factors:

$ Most trading volume is well under 35 million (and usually less than one million per day). If you held $10 000 worth of CRE at eight cents this would equate to 125 000 shares. If one million shares were traded on any one day by you and eight other people (who held the same number of shares as you), this would be a very small number. And it's highly likely that the other shareholders wouldn't want to buy and sell at the same prices. So, the chances of you buying at eight cents and selling at 10 cents for a 20 per cent profit is unlikely—let alone doubling your money.

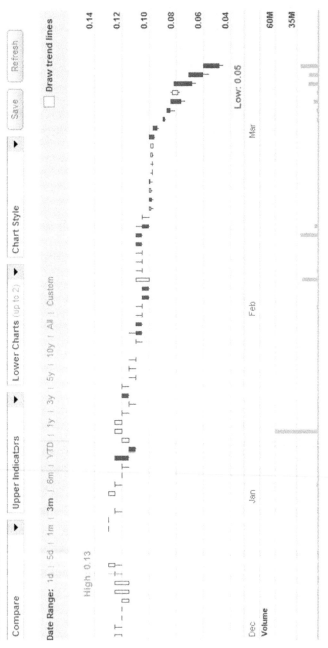

Figure 12.1: Crescent Gold candlestick chart for December 2010 to March 2011

Source: <www.CommSec.com.au>

$ There's increased volume as the share falls in price to under eight cents. This means many investors purchased higher—at 12 cents or even 10 cents—and are now having to sell at less than eight cents, halving their invested money.

It's just as hard to make 20 per cent on a cheap stock as it is on a much better known stock. So it's best to avoid penny stocks and invest in something much safer.

If I have $10 000 to invest, should I buy one or two stocks, or put $1000 into 10 different companies?

Great question, and really this answer will come down to how much you want to diversify. Buying into 10 different companies will spread your risk more, but it will usually also lower your return. And you need to take into account your brokerage costs, which on average would be $30 per trade and therefore it would cost $300 to buy shares in 10 different companies. You could keep that extra $270 for yourself (as you would only be paying for one trade) if you only purchased one company. It really depends on how risky or safe you want to be. However, if you do want more control and have done your research, I'd say two or three companies is ideal. I never hold more than six or so companies at any one time anyway because it can be too difficult to keep track of them all. If I had $10 000 to spend, I'd go for two or three companies.

 Lazy girl's guide to spreading your risk

If you do want to be safe and spread your risk around, buy into an index instead. You can buy all 20 stocks in the S&P/ASX 20 by buying XTL (the ASX 20 stock code). That way you can spread your risk by only having to pay for one brokerage transaction. Of course, that also means you can't pick and choose which companies you buy—you get all of the ones in the top 20 and that's it. However, it's a better option than trying to choose 10 (or 20) different companies yourself—and perfect if you're too lazy to do the research.

How do you know whether a stock is high or low risk?

Well, to be completely honest, all stocks are a risk. Of course, not as risky as placing all your money on the roulette table and hoping that number 14 will come up; nonetheless, there's still a real possibility that even with a perfectly good looking company you might lose some of your money.

However, as you've seen, some companies are a lot less risky than others. Usually you can find out by looking at things such as their earnings stability and comparing that to other companies within the sector, and also seeing what their five- or 10- year average return has been. (They have been listed for more than five years haven't they?)

Let's look at an example with CBA (Commonwealth Bank)—see figure 12.2.

Figure 12.2: earnings stability of CBA is 81.5 (as at April 2011)

ASX Code: CBA	Commonwealth Bank of Australia							
RISK		Company	All Ords	Sector ⓘ	Total Shareholder Return			
Beta		0.78	1.06	0.89	(avg annual rate)			
Earnings stability		81.5%		65.7%	1yr	3yr	5yr	10yr
Capital Adequacy ratio		11.49%		11.49%	-4.3%	13.2%	8.2%	11.8%
Net Impaired Assets		9.20%		11.85%				

Source: <www.CommSec.com.au>

Earnings stability can usually be found under the heading 'Risk' when you're researching a company. This company has an earnings stability of 81.5 per cent— very nice and stable, especially when you consider that other companies within that same sector are averaging an earnings stability of 65.7 per cent, CBA is a much lower risk than other similar shares.

You can also see that over the long term CBA has shown a very healthy return, which also makes it quite a safe bet. Yes, of course, anything can happen to CBA in the future, but right now things look positive for it.

Now let's look at another company within the same sector that doesn't seem quite so stable: SP AusNet (SPN)—see figure 12.3.

Figure 12.3: earnings stability of SPN is 47.9, which is lower than the sector average of 54.9 (as at April 2011)

ASX Code: SPN	SP AusNet							
RISK		Company	All Ords	Sector ▯	**Total Shareholder Return**			
Beta		1.00	1.06	0.79	(avg annual rate)			
Current ratio		1.03	1.72	1.20	1yr	3yr	5yr	10yr
Quick ratio		0.68	1.16	0.90	4.0%	0.1%	1.7%	--
Earnings stability		47.9%	54.9%	53.8%				
Debt/Equity ratio		161.5%	25.9%	62.8%				
Interest Cover		1.80	6.04	1.80				

Source: <www.CommSec.com.au>

As you can see, SP AusNet is a higher risk because its earnings stability is slightly lower than its sector average. It also hasn't performed brilliantly over the past five years, and while it wouldn't have lost you any money, it wouldn't have made you much either.

However, don't assume that just because a company has a high earnings stability it's going to make you money. It's good to remember that whatever it's done in the past, it will probably also do in the future.

How long should I hold a falling stock before I bail out?

Did you buy it following long-term or short-term rules? Generally, I'd consider bailing out of a stock if it fell 10 per cent or more. Arrange with your online broker to receive an SMS alert if the share price falls to a certain amount and then assess for yourself what it's doing.

Definitely sell if you purchased it on short-term rules, and put your sell price to 'market prices' so that you get out quickly.

If, however, you purchased the company using long-term rules, you need to assess the situation more closely. First, have a look across the board at all your stocks. Are they all falling or is just this one falling? If they're all falling it could be an indication of a small market crash and perhaps you'd feel safer if you just got out altogether and put your money in a nice, safe, high-interest account for a while. If just this company is falling, can you see a reason why? (Has it gone ex dividend? Has the CEO just been exposed for having an affair with his secretary?)

If it has gone ex dividend, then definitely keep it. It's likely to go back up in a few weeks. Generally, unless something major in the company has happened I'd continue to hold if the financials are still good. You don't want to panic sell if it's a good company. Even a scandal with the CEO (tsk tsk) isn't enough for me to want to bail—it will be old news in six or 12 months' time. Don't jump the fence even if all the other sheep do.

My best friend works at a major company and told me something that could affect the share price. What should I do?

Unfortunately, nothing. Don't buy (or if you already own some, sell) any shares. You could get done for insider trading. You might wonder if you'd even get noticed, being such a small investor, but generally all trading that happens prior to a major announcement will get a quick glance over by the ASX or ASIC. If trading seems suspicious, you might have to answer some tricky questions — and if they find out that your friend works for that company, then girl you have some 'splainin' to do.

I've been thinking about joining one of those investment clubs that give you a trading report or stock tips every week/month. Is this a good idea?

Ahh, the lazy girl's dream: having someone else do all the research for you and just give you a list of some of the best stocks to choose and trade with.

I have to come clean here and say that in the past I've actually been a member of one of these 'clubs'. It was a high-profile one and cost less than $1000 for a 12-month membership. At first I thought it was a great investment and when I was just beginning in the stock market I actually learned quite a lot because they explained why they made their decisions for choosing certain companies over others and everything seemed to make perfect sense.

However, after a few months I wasn't making the money I was expecting to make. Sure, some of the stocks they chose were winners, but I never made quite as much as the testimonials would have you believe.

If you think about it, if these sites have 1000 or more members (and many of them have *many* more than this), each trying to buy and sell on their recommendations, then no-one is going to make as much money as they could. As soon as a few people start buying (or selling), it's likely the price will move and you may not get in at the price they recommend, causing your profits to be reduced.

I'm not totally against these membership sites—some of them can be great education resources—but don't expect them to perform as well as they promise either.

In the end, I barely broke even so I decided to go it on my own instead. And the rest—as they say—is history.

Conclusion

You've finally reached the end of this book. I really hope you'll make millions in the market (even a few thousand would be nice!). That way your confidence in investing will grow and you'll probably begin to love the market as much as I do, or at least respect what it can do. And (ahem) I'll not be shy here: if you do make a ton of money, please recommend my book to your friends so they buy a copy too. My dream is to help every woman become more financially savvy, to have freedom of choice and, of course, to have more shopping money at her disposal.

When I started out investing in the market I certainly didn't consider myself all that talented in choosing the right stocks. I chopped and changed strategies often and every time one strategy didn't seem to work I'd switch to the next. I was on the search for the Holy Grail of strategies that would guarantee me untold wealth (I told you I dreamed a lot, didn't I?).

What I didn't realise then is that no one strategy will work 100 per cent of the time; that's why there are so many different methods (just take a look at the number of sharemarket books on the shelves of your nearest bookstore and you'll know what I mean). What I wished I had known early on is that most good investment strategies, when followed diligently, *do* work, so find the one that suits you best. It's a bit like dieting: while there are so many different ways to lose weight—combine foods, exclude carbs or whatever the latest fad is—when it comes down to it there's really only one true formula for losing weight and that's to expend more energy (calories) than you eat. It's basic mathematics. It's the same with shares: there's no magic strategy that's the winning formula—it comes down to basic maths and a good investment plan.

Eventually, after trial and error, I finally figured out what I was doing and everything seemed to fall into place. My income was going up more often than it was going down and I was starting to actually make money at this stock market thing. And, yes, I was having fun along the way (come on, it's fun to watch your share double in price in just a few months). You certainly don't need to be a maths genius or business professional to invest in the stock market; anyone from your high-school geek to your pink-lip-gloss-wearing diva has the potential to be financially successful in the market with a little research and patience.

The most important rule (and one I hope you've learned from this book because I've tried to mention it a zillion times) is that cutting your losses early and letting your profits run is the real key to making money on the stock market. Let me repeat the magic rule: *cut your losses early, and let your profits ride*. It's not finding the magic stock that will make your fortune (although if you do, let me know *your* strategy!); it's having a consistent investment plan that you stick with and (yes, I'm going to say it again) cut your losses early if your shares go against you. Avoiding losses is the key to gaining profits. Not every share you own will be a winner, so dump the losers and keep those stocks that earn you a nice little profit.

Throughout this book I've let you in on my best strategies for both long- and short-term investing—strategies that have consistently made me money in both slow and fast markets and that I still use now to help keep me in the investing game. I've made some good profits using them, and I hope you will too.

Good luck, and I wish you a happy, profitable future—no prince required.

Index

Also by Tracey Edwards

Available from all good bookstores

Lightning Source UK Ltd.
Milton Keynes UK
UKHW022226080620
364668UK00008B/731